TAX POLICY AND THE ECONOMY 10

edited by **James M. Poterba**

National Bureau of Economic Research
The MIT Press, Cambridge, Massachusetts

Send orders and business correspondence to:
The MIT Press
55 Hayward Street
Cambridge, MA 02142

In the United Kingdom, continental Europe, and the Middle East and Africa, send orders and business correspondence to:
The MIT Press Ltd.
Fitzroy House, 11 Chenies Street
London WC1E 7ET
ENGLAND

ISSN: 9892-8649
ISBN: hardcover 0-262-16161-3
       paperback 0-262-66098-9

Copyright Information
Permission to photocopy articles for internal or personal use, or the internal or personal use of specific clients, is granted by the copyright owner for users registered with the Copyright Clearance Center (CCC) Transactional Reporting Service, provided that the fee of $10.00 per copy is paid directly to CCC, 222 Rosewood Drive, Danvers, MA 01923. The fee code for users of the Transactional Reporting Service is: 0892-8649/96 $10.00. For those organizations that have been granted a photocopy license with CCC, a separate system of payment has been arranged.

© 1996 by the National Bureau of Economic Research and The Massachusetts Institute of Technology.

NATIONAL BUREAU OF ECONOMIC RESEARCH

Officers:
Paul W. McCracken, *Chairman*
John H. Biggs, *Vice Chairman*
Martin Feldstein, *President and Chief Executive Officer*
Gerald A. Polansky, *Treasurer*
Sam Parker, *Director of Finance and Corporate Secretary*
Susan Colligan, *Assistant Corporate Secretary*
Deborah Mankiw, *Assistant Corporate Secretary*

Directors at Large:

Peter C. Aldrich	George C. Eads	Robert T. Parry
Elizabeth E. Bailey	Martin Feldstein	Peter G. Peterson
John H. Biggs	George Hatsopoulos	Richard N. Rosett
Andrew Brimmer	Karen N. Horn	Bert Seidman
Carl F. Christ	Lawrence R. Klein	Kathleen P. Utgoff
Don R. Conlan	Leo Melamed	Donald S. Wasserman
Kathleen B. Cooper	Merton H. Miller	Marina v. N. Whitman
Jean A. Crockett	Michael H. Moskow	John O. Wilson

Directors by University Appointment:

George Akerlof, *California, Berkeley*
Jagdish Bhagwati, *Columbia*
William C. Brainard, *Yale*
Glen G. Cain, *Wisconsin*
Franklin Fisher, *Massachusetts Institute of Technology*
Saul H. Hymans, *Michigan*
Marjorie B. McElroy, *Duke*
Joel Mokyr, *Northwestern*
Andrew Postlewaite, *Pennsylvania*
Nathan Rosenberg, *Stanford*
Harold T. Shapiro, *Princeton*
Craig Swan, *Minnesota*
David B. Yoffie, *Harvard*
Arnold Zellner, *Chicago*

Directors by Appointment of Other Organizations:

Marcel Boyer, *Canadian Economics Association*
Mark Drabenstott, *American Agricultural Economics Association*
William C. Dunkelberg, *National Association of Business Economists*
Richard A. Easterlin, *Economic History Association*
Gail D. Fosler, *The Conference Board*
A. Ronald Gallant, *American Statistical Association*
Robert S. Hamada, *American Finance Association*
Charles Lave, *American Economic Association*
Rudolph A. Oswald, *American Federation of Labor and Congress of Industrial Organizations*
Gerald A. Polansky, *American Institute of Certified Public Accountants*
Josh S. Weston, *Committee for Economic Development*

Directors Emeriti:

Moses Abramovitz	Paul W. McCracken	Eli Shapiro
George T. Conklin, Jr.	Geoffrey H. Moore	William S. Vickrey
Thomas D. Flynn	James J. O'Leary	
Franklin A. Lindsay	George B. Roberts	

Since this volume is a record of conference proceedings, it has been exempted from the rules governing critical review of manuscripts by the Board of Directors of the National Bureau (resolution adopted 8 June 1948, as revised 21 November 1949 and 20 April 1968).

CONTENTS

Introduction *James M. Poterba* vii

Acknowledgments xi

PRIVATIZATION OF SOCIAL SECURITY: HOW IT WORKS AND WHY IT MATTERS 1
Laurence J. Kotlikoff

WHY HAVE SEPARATE ENVIRONMENTAL TAXES? 33
Don Fullerton

THE EFFECTS OF TAX REFORM ON PRICES AND ASSET VALUES 71
Robert E. Hall

THE EFFECT OF INCREASED TAX RATES ON TAXABLE INCOME AND ECONOMIC EFFICIENCY: A PRELIMINARY ANALYSIS OF THE 1993 TAX RATE INCREASES 89
Martin Feldstein and Daniel Feenberg

TAX REFORMS AND LABOR SUPPLY 119
Nada Eissa

INTRODUCTION

James M. Poterba
MIT and NBER

Just after the passage of the Tax Reform Act of 1986, the NBER inaugurated an annual conference designed to facilitate an exchange of ideas between public finance scholars and those in industry and government who are directly involved in the tax policy-making process. The Tax Policy and the Economy conference, which celebrates its tenth anniversary this year, is devoted to the presentation of new research findings of relevance for tax policy analysts.

Fundamental changes in federal tax and expenditure policies appear more likely today than at any point in the last 10 years. Discussions of drastically changing or even eliminating the federal income tax, and of far-reaching changes in major federal entitlement programs, have moved from the fringes to the center of the national policy agenda. The outcomes of these current debates are uncertain, but it is clear that this is a critical moment for research input to the policy-design process. The five papers in this volume represent a cross section of some of the best applied research that bears on current deliberations about tax and expenditure policy. Each paper provides new data and new insights on an important policy issue.

The first paper, "Privatization of Social Security: How It Works and Why It Matters," by Laurence J. Kotlikoff, is directed at a broad class of proposals for social security reform. Kotlikoff first describes the key elements of any proposal that would replace the current pay-as-you-go social security system with a system of mandatory private retirement savings accounts. He then uses a dynamic general equilibrium model, with parameter values chosen for rough consistency with the current U.S. economy, to evaluate the economic consequences of privatization.

The paper considers the short-term and long-term effects of privatization on capital accumulation, on the level of aggregate output, and on the relative well-being of individuals in different generations. The results show that privatization can generate long-run increases in output and per capita income, but that individuals who are alive at the time of the privatization may be worse off as a result of these reforms. The paper also succeeds in identifying a number of research issues where further work is needed both in designing privatization proposals and in evaluating their effects.

Don Fullerton's paper, "Why Have Separate Environmental Taxes?," compares the structure of current U.S. environmental excise taxes with the types of taxes that optimal tax design principles would dictate. Fullerton concludes that existing taxes, which are typically levied at low rates relative to the value of the taxed products, impose high administrative costs relative to the revenue they collect. He also observes that these taxes are not levied on the basis of any objective measure of the environmental damage. Thus, the current tax structure bears little resemblance to the optimal tax structure that would result from including an explicit consideration of environmental damage in a standard tax design framework.

The third paper, by Robert E. Hall, provides a comprehensive summary entitled "The Effects of Tax Reform on Prices and Asset Values." This paper considers a range of consumption tax alternatives to the current personal income tax, including value-added taxes, retail sales taxes, a progressive consumed income tax, and the Hall–Rabushka flat tax proposal. Hall considers how each of these proposals would affect the price level, the real wages earned by workers and paid by firms, the market value of existing assets, and the saving and investment incentives facing households and firms. The paper clarifies much of the previous discussion on each of these topics and highlights the behavioral parameters that are the central determinants of the effects of fundamental tax reform. It also emphasizes differences between the alternative methods of implementing a consumption tax, particularly in the adjustments to nominal wages and nominal prices that would be required to restore equilibrium after tax reform.

Martin Feldstein and Daniel Feenberg's paper, "The Effect of Increased Tax Rates on Taxable Income and Economic Efficiency: A Preliminary Analysis of the 1993 Tax Rate Increases," presents a preliminary analysis of the revenue consequences of the 1993 increase in marginal tax rates on high-income households. This tax increase raised the top marginal income tax rate from 31% to 39.6% for households with taxable incomes in excess of $250,000 and from 31% to 36% for those with incomes between $140,000 ($115,000 for single filers) and $250,000. Feldstein and Feenberg compare preliminary information from Internal Revenue Service data on 1993 taxable income reported by taxpayers in different taxable income classes with comparable data from 1992. They conclude that 1993 taxable income for the highest income groups was substantially less than one would have expected on the basis of this group's 1992 taxable income and the overall rate of economic expansion between 1992 and 1993. While definitive measurement of the revenue effects of the 1993 tax bill requires panel data on the taxable income of the same individual in several different years, the Feldstein–Feenberg results suggest that the 1993 tax reform may have raised less revenue than at least some analysts expected it to. If the revenue gain from the 1993 act was small, then its efficiency cost is likely to have been high because the act substantially raised marginal tax rates for high-income households.

The last paper, Nada Eissa's study, "Tax Reforms and Labor Supply," describes the evidence on how taxation affects labor supply that has emerged from recent studies of U.S. income tax reforms. The paper begins by describing the author's previous work on taxation and labor supply. This includes work on how the Economic Recovery Tax Act of 1981 and the Tax Reform Act of 1986 (TRA) affected the labor supply of married women and on how revision of the Earned Income Tax Credit (EITC) rules in the early 1990s affected labor supply. The evidence for both the TRA and the EITC suggests a substantial labor force participation and hours-of-work response by women whose after-tax wage rates increase as a result of tax policy. Eissa's paper complements this summary of previous work by presenting new evidence on the effect of the 1981 and 1986 tax reforms on men's labor supply. The evidence suggests relatively small tax effects, if any, on men.

The papers in this volume contribute to a continuing and improving interaction between academics and policymakers concerned with tax policy. In some cases they reflect suggestions of previous Tax Policy and the Economy conference participants with respect to topic choice. In others they represent an attempt to bring current research, and the scholars who are conducting it, into close proximity with the policymaking community. The number of participants in the Washington meeting at which these papers were presented exceeded that at any previous Tax Policy and the Economy meeting. This provides at least some testimony to the value that industry and government tax policy experts place on the dialogue that this conference permits.

ACKNOWLEDGMENTS

Many individuals played a key role in planning and organizing this tenth annual NBER meeting on Tax Policy and the Economy. Martin Feldstein, President of the NBER, was a key proponent of these meetings at their beginning, and he has been an active supporter of this annual conference throughout the last decade. Deborah Mankiw, the NBER's Director of Corporate and Foundation Relations, and Liz Cary helped throughout the conference planning process. The NBER Conference Department, particularly Conference Director Kirsten Foss Davis and Lauren Lariviere, managed the daunting task of ensuring that the papers were prepared and distributed in a timely fashion and handled the complex logistics for a large but very efficient conference in Washington, D.C. Deborah Kiernan shepherded the manuscripts through the prepublication process with her usual speed and attention to detail.

I am also grateful to Deputy Treasury Secretary Lawrence Summers, who spoke at the conference luncheon and reflected on developments in U.S. tax policy in the 10 years since he organized the first Tax Policy and the Economy meeting.

Finally, I wish to thank each of the authors whose papers are included in this volume for striving to communicate their important research findings to a largely nonacademic audience. I appreciate their efforts and willingness to participate in this very important opportunity for interchange between academics and policymakers.

PRIVATIZATION OF SOCIAL SECURITY: HOW IT WORKS AND WHY IT MATTERS

Laurence J. Kotlikoff
Boston University and NBER

EXECUTIVE SUMMARY

This paper uses the Auerbach–Kotlikoff dynamic life-cycle model (AK model) to examine the macroeconomic and efficiency effects of privatizing social security. It also uses a simple privatization proposal, the Personal Security System, as a framework to discuss a number of other issues associated with privatizing social security, including transition rules and changes in the overall degree of progressivity.

According to the AK model's simulations, privatizing social security can generate very major long-run increases in output and living standards. These gains come largely, but not exclusively, at the expense of existing generations. Indeed, the pure efficiency gains from privatization can be substantial. The term efficiency gains refers here to the welfare improvement available to future generations after existing generations have been fully compensated for their losses from privatization. The precise size of the efficiency gain depends on the existing tax structure, the linkage between benefits and taxes under the existing social security system, and the choice of the tax instrument used to finance benefits during the transition.

Laurence J. Kotlikoff is Professor of Economics at Boston University and a Research Associate of the NBER. I thank Jan Walliser for excellent research assistance and Peter Diamond, Henry Aaron, and Jan Walliser for very helpful comments.

When the initial tax structure features a progressive income tax, when the existing system's benefit–tax linkage is low, when consumption taxation is used to finance social security benefits during the transition, and when existing generations are fully compensated for their privatization losses, there is a 4.5 percent simulated welfare gain to future generations from privatization. However, if these circumstances do not hold, the efficiency gains from privatization are likely to be smaller, possibly even negative. For example, when the initial tax structure is a proportional income tax, when the benefit–tax linkage is perceived to be dollar for dollar, when the income tax rate is increased to finance social security benefits during the privatization transition, and when current generations are fully compensated, there is a 3.1 percent welfare loss to future generations.

The illustrative Personal Security System shows that there are simple ways to privatize the retirement portion of the U.S. Social Security System and to credit workers for their past social security contributions. It also suggests that privatizing social security could provide more survivor protection than the current system as well as eliminate much of the current system's seemingly capricious redistribution between two-earner and single-earner couples. But the proposal's analysis also suggests that these benefits from privatization must be set against a possible reduction in progressivity and a likely reduction in the amount of longevity insurance available to the elderly through annuities.

1. INTRODUCTION

Privatization of social security is spreading around the world. Chile's highly publicized and successful privatization was the first in a growing list that includes, or will soon include, privatizations in Argentina, Australia, Bolivia, Columbia, Mexico, Peru, and the United Kingdom. Will the United States join this club? Should it, on economic grounds? If it does join, what form might its privatization take?

This paper does not predict whether social security will be privatized in the United States, nor what form such privatization might take. Instead, it lays out the macroeconomic issues involved in privatizing Social Security, uses the Auerbach–Kotlikoff dynamic fiscal policy model (AK model) to simulate the macroeconomic and efficiency effects of privatization, and shows, by means of an actual proposal, that the U.S. system could be privatized in a simple and straightforward manner. The proposal considered is entitled the Personal Security System. Its analysis will help to clarify some of the microeconomic issues involved in privatizing social security.

This is not the first paper to consider many of these issues, nor is it the first to simulate social security privatizations. Feldstein (1995) uses a partial equilibrium framework, and Arrau (1990) and Arrau and Schmidt-Hebbel (1993) use a version of the AK model to make a number of the points argued here. The AK model used by Arrau (1990) and Arrau and Schmidt-Hebbel (1993) takes labor supply as exogenous. This is a significant shortcoming, since the efficiency gains from privatizing social security arise, in large part, from eliminating social security's distortion of labor supply decisions. Raffelhueschen (1993) does include variable labor supply in his simulation analysis of privatizing social security, and his qualitative conclusions are quite similar to those reached here. But Raffelhueschen's model contains only two periods, which limits the applicability of his quantitative findings. Like this study, Imrohoroglu, Huang, and Sargent (1995) use a multiperiod life-cycle model to simulate the effects of privatizing social security. Although their model is more elaborate than that used here, it does not include variable labor supply, which precludes separating efficiency gains from intergenerational redistribution. Nonetheless, their general findings concerning noncompensated social security privatization transitions accord with those presented here.

2. PRIVATIZATION OF SOCIAL SECURITY AND THE MACROECONOMY

Most industrialized economies and a good many developing countries have spent the postwar period dramatically expanding their pay-as-you-go social security programs. Although this expansion has reduced poverty rates among the elderly, it has also redistributed tremendous sums from young and future generations, as a group, to contemporaneous older generations, as a group.

The mechanism underlying the redistribution to the initial elderly is clear. Generations that are retired or close to retirement at the time that pay-as-you-go social security benefits are increased receive windfalls. The mechanism underlying the redistribution away from younger and future generations is less clear, at least to the general public. The public understands that expanding pay-as-you-go social security means higher payroll taxes for current and future young workers, but it also sees the higher benefits these generations will, themselves, receive when they retire. What the public misses is that the present value of the social security benefits that these generations will receive is far less than the present value of the taxes they will pay once one discounts these flows at prevailing pretax returns to domestic and foreign capital. Stated differently, the public misses the fact that the implicit rate of return paid on social security contributions in a mature system is far less than the return available on investments in the international economy.

The public also misses the major macroeconomic effects of these programs, which are to raise the consumption of the elderly, lower national savings and investment, and, as a result, raise real interest rates and reduce real wage rates relative to what they would otherwise have been. These general equilibrium feedback effects exacerbate the redistribution from young and future generations to the initial old (see Auerbach and Kotlikoff, 1987). This is not just a theoretical possibility. As Gokhale, Kotlikoff, and Sabelhaus (1996) show, the dramatic postwar decline in U.S. savings has coincided with a dramatic increase in the absolute and relative consumption of the elderly, which, in turn, can be traced to the U.S. government's postwar intergenerational redistribution.

2.1 Demographic Strains

The fiscal burdening of young and future generations through pay-as-you-go social security can occur just as well in settings with stable and unstable demographics. But a baby boom followed by a baby bust of the kind recently experienced by most developed economies places added stress on the social security chain letter. Indeed, the United States, Japan, Germany, Italy, France, and a host of other countries now face the unpleasant prospect of either dramatically raising their payroll tax rates over the next few decades or dramatically reducing their social security benefits. It is this impending demographic/social security crunch, rather than a real appreciation of the intrinsic problem with running unfunded social security programs, that is leading politicians to consider privatizing social security.

Many politicians appear to believe that privatizing social security represents a painless way out of their country's demographic dilemmas. This will not necessarily be the case. When potential efficiency gains from privatizing social security are ignored, fiscal policy is, generationally speaking, a zero-sum game. Consequently, if privatization is used to mitigate the prospective increase in the fiscal burden on future generations, it is likely to do so at the price of a higher fiscal burden on current generations.[1]

2.2 Zero-Sum Generational Accounting

Equation (1) makes this last point clear. Equation (1) is the government's intertemporal budget constraint:

[1] This statement takes as given the government's projected path of purchases of goods and services.

$$N_{-100} + N_{-99} + \cdots + N_0 + N_1 + N_2 + \cdots + N_\infty = G_0 + D_0. \tag{1}$$

where N_t represents all net taxes (taxes paid minus transfer payments received) to be paid in current and future years by the generation born in year t, where the present year is indexed as 0. N_{-100} is the remaining net taxes to be paid by those born 100 years ago; N_{-99} is the net taxes to be paid by those born 99 years ago; N_0 represents the net taxes to be paid by current newborns (those born in year 0); and N_1, N_2, and N_∞ are the net taxes to be paid by those who will be born in years 1, 2, and the indefinite future, respectively. All the net tax terms are measured as actuarial present values.

The term G_0 represents the present value, as of year 0, of the government's current and future purchases of goods and services; and D_0 represents the government's official net debt (its official liabilities less official assets) in year 0. The discount rate used to form the N_t values as well as the value of G_0 is the economy-wide marginal product of capital. This budget constraint tells us that net tax payments of current and future generations must collectively cover the government's bills, given by $G_0 + D_0$. It also tells us that if the size of the government's bills is held constant, any reduction in the net tax payments of one generation requires an increase in the net tax payments of one or more other generations.

From the perspective of equation (1), introducing pay-as-you-go social security lowers the N_t values of those above a certain age, say 40, but raises the N_t values of those below that age as well as those not yet born. This reflects the fact that the N_t values include the present value of future social security contributions minus the present value of future social security benefits. In our example, since the social security benefits received by generations under age 40 are smaller, when discounted at the internationally available pretax return to capital, than are their tax contributions, pay-as-you-go social security raises their N_t values.

Now suppose the objective of privatizing social security is to lower the fiscal burden on all future generations, that is, to lower the N_t values for all generations born after year 0. Also suppose that privatization does not entail a decline in the government's future purchases, which would lower G_0. Then the government's budget constraint insists that the N_t values of one or more currently living generations will have to increase.

To make this concrete, suppose that the government privatizes social security by (1) allowing workers to make their social security contributions to private pensions, (2) making up for the loss in social security revenue by raising consumption taxes, and (3) gradually cutting benefits of new retirees. Since retired elderly pay consumption taxes, but do not make social security contributions, this method of privatizing social security raises the N_t values of those who are old at the time of the privatization. The consumption tax increase as well as the cuts in social security benefits are also likely to raise the N_t values of initial younger generations. The net impact of this is a reduction in the N_t values of those not yet born. If, instead of raising consumption taxes, the government makes up for its lost revenue through official borrowing, but uses, say, the income tax to cover interest payments on this additional official debt, the result will be similar. In this case, the N_t values of the initial elderly will rise because they pay a larger share of income taxes than they do of social security payroll taxes.

2.3 The Effects of Privatization on Savings, Investment, and Economic Growth

According to the life-cycle model, changes in the N_t values will affect savings, investment, and economic growth. The reason is that older generations have a larger propensity to consume than do younger ones, and younger ones, in turn, have higher a propensity to consume than do future generations, whose current propensity to consume is zero. By lowering the N_t values of initial young and future generations and raising those of initial older generations, privatizing social security produces *income effects* that lower aggregate consumption and, thereby, raise aggregate saving, investment, and, at least temporarily, economic growth.

But privatizing social security may also change saving incentives in a way that discourages saving. Take, for example, the case that income tax finance is used to pay for interest on debt issued to privatize social security. The higher effective rate of capital income taxation that results from higher income tax rates raises the price of consuming in the future relative to the present and provides the young and old alike with an incentive to substitute current for future consumption (i.e., to save less).[2] Such *substitution effects* on current consumption may outweigh privatization's income effects, producing a net increase in consumption and a concomitant decline in national savings, investment, and, at least temporarily, economic growth.

Since the savings, investment, and economic growth effects of privatizing social security are theoretically ambiguous, depending on how privatization is conducted, simulation analysis is needed to understand the net macroeconomic impact of privatization. Before turning to such analysis, let us consider other issues involved in privatizing social security.

---

[2] Changes in the relative of price of current and future consumption may also produce income effects, unless households are compensated for such relative price changes.

2.4 Are There Efficiency Gains from Privatizing Social Security?

Our discussion of the zero-sum nature of privatizing social security is abstracted from the issue of economic efficiency. Economic efficiency concerns the structure of economic incentives, such as the incentive to consume now rather than later and the incentive to work rather than take leisure. Since privatization of social security will generally alter economic incentives, the possibility arises that privatization could make the economy more efficient. In technical terms, improving the economy's efficiency means being able to make some people better off without hurting others. In our context, it means making some generations better off through privatization without leaving others worse off.

Whether or not privatizing social security improves efficiency depends on the nature of the pre-privatization linkage, at the margin, between social security benefits and contributions. This linkage could, of course, be zero. Zero linkage occurs when social security benefits are determined independent of past contributions or when workers incorrectly perceive that their additional social security contributions will not raise their future social security benefits. In the United States, misconception of the true nature of benefit–tax linkage seems plausible given the complex nature of our social security benefit calculation.

In a "pay-as-you-go" system with zero actual or perceived linkage, workers will consider 100 percent of their payroll tax contribution to be a marginal tax on their labor supply. Nonetheless, in a pay-as-you go program with stable growth, workers will on average receive some return on their contributions to social security, a return that is governed by the rate of growth of the economy. So, on average, social security contributions are not just a tax.

This point notwithstanding, there is no necessary relationship between the average and marginal returns to social security contributions. To see this, suppose that the social security payroll tax rate is 15 percent. If benefits are provided as a lump sum independent of past contributions, the marginal return from an extra dollar of contributions is zero, and social security adds 15 percentage points to the total effective marginal tax rate on labor supply. If, on the other hand, the government provides, in present value, $2 for every dollar contributed to social security above some contribution level, then social security will represent a marginal subsidy to the labor supply—one that reduces the total effective marginal tax rate on labor supply by 15 percentage points.[3]

The smaller is a social security system's marginal benefit–tax linkage,

---

[3] This assumes that all workers contribute above this contribution level.

the larger are the chances that privatizing social security can support an efficiency gain. To see this, consider a pre-privatization situation in which social security benefits are provided to workers independent of their past contributions, so that the marginal linkage is zero, and workers view all their payroll tax contributions as a marginal tax on their labor supply. Also assume that privatization is effected by paying only those social security benefits owed to existing retirees as well as those benefits that current workers have accrued as of the date of the privatization. In this case, the payroll tax will, over time, disappear as a smaller and smaller number of original retirees and workers with accrued benefits remain alive. As the payroll tax rate falls, the total effective tax on labor supply will fall as well. Since the government's distortion of labor supply is reduced over time, this method of privatizing social security has the potential of improving economic efficiency.

Note that lowering effective marginal tax rates on labor supply can also be accomplished under the existing social security system by simply tightening the link between benefits received and contributions paid; that is, the fact that social security is financed at the macrolevel on a pay-as-you-go basis does not preclude establishing a tight and transparent linkage between social security benefits and contributions—a linkage that, at the margin, can, as mentioned, even entail an effective subsidy to labor supply.[4]

Privatizing social security can also reduce economic efficiency. To see this, take the case that social security subsidizes labor supply at the margin and thereby reduces the total effective marginal labor income tax rate. In this case, privatizing social security in the manner just described will eliminate this marginal subsidy, raising the effective marginal tax on labor supply and reducing economic efficiency.

In addition to its impact on effective marginal tax rates on labor supply, privatization may also alter other effective marginal tax rates. For example, if privatization is accomplished by using income tax finance to pay, over time, the accrued benefits owed to current retirees and workers with no subsequent benefit accrual, there will be a temporary increase in effective marginal capital income taxation. If effective marginal capital income taxation is already quite high due to, say, a high corporate income tax, privatization could well reduce economic efficiency.

Thus, there is no guarantee that privatizing social security will improve economic efficiency. It all depends on the type of social security

---

[4] For an analysis of the efficiency gains from tightening the linkage between social security benefits and contributions, see Chapter 10 in Auerbach and Kotlikoff (1987).

system being privatized, the nature of other fiscal distortions, and the manner in which privatization takes place.

3. ILLUSTRATING SOCIAL SECURITY PRIVATIZATION EFFECTS WITH THE AUERBACH–KOTLIKOFF MODEL

The Auerbach–Kotlikoff (AK) model can provide some sense of the potential saving, investment, and growth effects of privatizing social security.[5] The AK model calculates the time path of all economic variables in its economy over a 150-year period. The model has 55 overlapping generations. Each adult agent in the model lives for 55 years (from age 20 to age 75).

There are three sectors: households, firms, and the government. Households (adult agents) decide how much to work and how much to save based on the after-tax wages and after-tax rates of return they can earn in the present and the future on their labor supply and savings, respectively. The work decision involves not only deciding how much to work in those years that one is working, but also when to retire. The AK model's consumption and leisure preferences that underlie these decisions were chosen in light of evidence on actual labor supply and saving behavior.

As agents age in the model, they experience a realistic profile of increases in wages. This age–wage profile is separate from the general level of wages, the time path of which is determined in solving the model. Fiscal policies affect households by altering their after-tax wages, their after-tax rates of return, and, in the case of consumption taxes, their after-tax prices of goods and services. The model is equipped to deal with income taxes, wage taxes, capital income taxes, and consumption taxes. It is also able to handle progressive as well as proportional tax rates. Finally, and most important for this study, the model includes a pay-as-you-go social security system in which the perceived linkage between taxes and benefits can be set at any desired value.

All agents are assumed to have the same preferences, so differences in behavior across agents arise solely from differences in economic opportunities. Since all agents within an age cohort are assumed to be identical, differences in economic opportunities are present only across cohorts. In this study, the model's population growth rate is set at a constant 1

---

[5] For a detailed description of the AK model, see Auerbach and Kotlikoff (1987).

percent rate, with the population of each new cohort being 1 percent larger than that of the previous cohort.

The AK model's production sector is characterized by perfectly competitive firms that hire labor and capital to maximize their profits. The production relationships that underlie firms' hiring decisions and their production of output are based on empirical findings for the United States. The government sector consists of a Treasury that collects resources from the private sector to finance government consumption and an unfunded, "pay-as-you-go" Social Security system that levies payroll taxes to pay for contemporaneous retiree benefit payments. There is no money in the model, and, thus, no monetary policy. There is, however, government debt, and the model can handle deficit-financed reductions in payroll and other taxes. It can also handle gradual phaseins of one tax for the other. Finally, the model contains a Lump-Sum Redistribution Authority (LSRA), a hypothetical governmental agency that can use lump-sum taxes and transfers to redistribute among generations alive at a point in time as well as those who will be born in the future. The LSRA can be used (switched on) to study the pure economic efficiency effects of particular policy changes.

Although the model handles a great number of complex processes, it leaves out large portions of reality. The model's agents are heterogeneous only with respect to their age. There are no welfare recipients or millionaires whose saving and work behavior might differ dramatically from that of the model's agents. The model does not include saving for purposes other than retirement, such as bequests. Nor does the model incorporate uncertainty either with respect to individual or macroeconomic outcomes. These and other omissions suggest viewing the model's results cautiously.

3.1 Modeling the Privatization of Social Security

In the AK model, privatizing social security contributions is simple. It just requires setting the model's social security payroll tax rate to zero. Since agents in the model are free to dissave (borrow) as well as to save (lend/invest), forcing them to contribute to private pensions will make no difference to their total savings and consumption; that is, forced private pension savings will simply crowd out voluntary private savings dollar for dollar. Hence, there is no need to add a formal private pension system to the model.

Privatizing social security benefits within the model involves three key decisions: (1) how fast to phase out benefits; (2) whether to issue explicit government debt for a period of time to make up for some or all of the loss in payroll tax revenue; and (3) what tax instrument to use, during the benefit phaseout period, to pay for benefits that are not financed by explicit borrowing and to meet, during and after the benefit phaseout period, interest on new debt issued as part of the privatization.

These three decisions are illustrated in Chile's privatization of social security. Chile's privatization honored benefit commitments to existing retirees. It also provided existing workers with *recognition bonds*—explicit IOUs that would come due when they reached retirement age. These recognition bonds compensated the workers for the elimination of their claims to future social security benefits, claims that they had accrued as a result of past contributions. Because the timing of the payment of principal and interest on the recognition bonds is similar to the timing of the payment of the accrued social security benefits that these workers would otherwise have received, the Chilean reform can be viewed as paying off all accrued benefits under the old system but disallowing any further accrual of social security benefits. Consequently, it amounts to a particular benefit phaseout policy. Chile used deficit finance to cover some of the losses in revenue arising from the discontinuation of the payroll tax. This deficit finance took the form of running smaller surpluses than would otherwise have been the case. Finally, Chile used its income tax to make up the rest of the lost payroll tax revenue and, implicitly, to meet interest payments on its additional borrowing.

3.2 The AK Model Used to Study Privatization of Social Security

The AK model's steady state from which privatizations of social security are simulated features a 20 percent income tax, a pay-as-you-go social security system with a 12 percent payroll tax rate, a marginal benefit–tax linkage of zero, zero initial explicit debt, a 1 percent population growth rate, zero technological change, and a Cobb–Douglas production function. Social security benefits equal 75 percent of the average level of wages earned between ages 1 and 45 (real world ages of 20 and 65). The intertemporal and intratemporal elasticities of substitution in the Consumer Expenditure Survey (CES) utility function are set at the conservative values of 0.25 and 0.8, respectively. Households have a pure rate of time preference of 1.5 percent per year, and the initial steady-state interest rate is 9.1 percent. The base-case simulation begins in year 1 and involves (1) an immediate elimination of the payroll tax, (2) a 45-year phaseout of security benefits starting in year 11, and (3) the use of income tax finance to make up for the loss in payroll tax revenues in meeting social security benefit payments.

Delaying the benefit phaseout for 10 years ensures that all retirees collecting benefits at the time of the reform (all those 46 to 55 years old) receive all the benefits they had been promised. Spending 45 years phasing out social security benefits ensures that all workers alive at the time of the reform receive some social security benefits when they retire. The phaseout of benefits is linear over the 45-year period, but more rapid or slower phaseouts can be considered. In terms of the Chilean privatization, the rapidity of the benefit phaseout captures the choice of discount rate, survival rates, and other factors used in determining the size of recognition bonds given to existing workers.

The reduction in the payroll tax burden facing future generations combines with the increase in the real wage to raise the utility of those born in the long run by 9.7 percent. This is a very significant long-run welfare improvement, but it comes at a price. As the lower panel in Figure 1 shows, initial generations are made worse off; 30-year olds suffer the largest percent reduction in their remaining utility, 2.0 percent.

3.3 Can Privatization Improve Economic Efficiency?

The utility changes in Figure 1 beg the question of whether, in the course of privatizing social security, initial generations can be compensated by future generations, leaving them no worse off and future generations better off. Such an outcome, referred to as a *Pareto improvement*, is clearly more efficient than the initial steady-state status quo.

Figure 2 answers this question in the affirmative. It shows the results of running the base-case privatization simulation but with the LSRA instructed to redistribute across generations in a nondistorting manner to (1) leave each initial generation at its preprivatization level of utility, and (2) leave each generation born after the reform with the same level of utility. It is important to note that the LSRA's activities are fully incorporated into the model; that is, the model's agents take into account the lump-sum net taxes (which may be negative) that they must pay to the LSRA. Moreover, the requisite size of these generation-specific net transfers are calculated simultaneously with all the other variables in the model in solving for the economy's dynamic general equilibrium.

3.4 Base-Case Results

The results of the base case and other nine simulations considered in this section are presented in Tables 1 to 5. For each simulation, there is also a figure with two panels. The top panel shows how indices of the capital stock, output, the wage, and the interest rate change during the privatization transition. The lower panel shows the impact of privatization on generations alive at the time of the reform and thereafter. The horizontal axis in the lower panel indicates the year in which the various generations were born, and the vertical axis provides an index of the generation's utility levels. A value of 1.06 means that the genera-

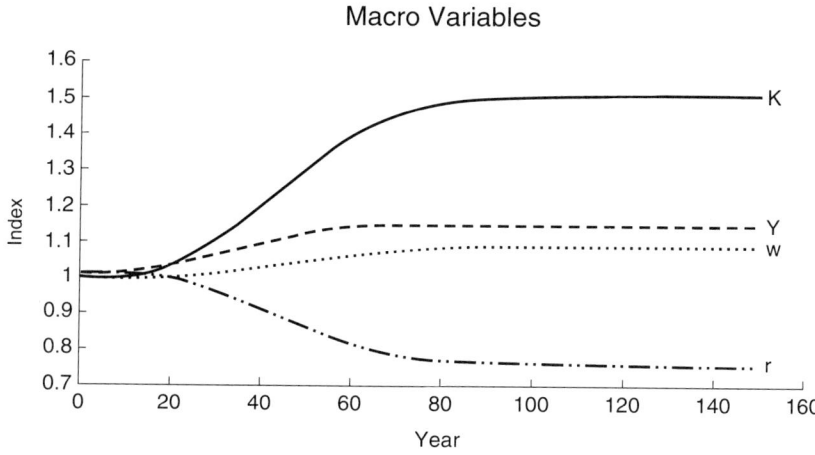

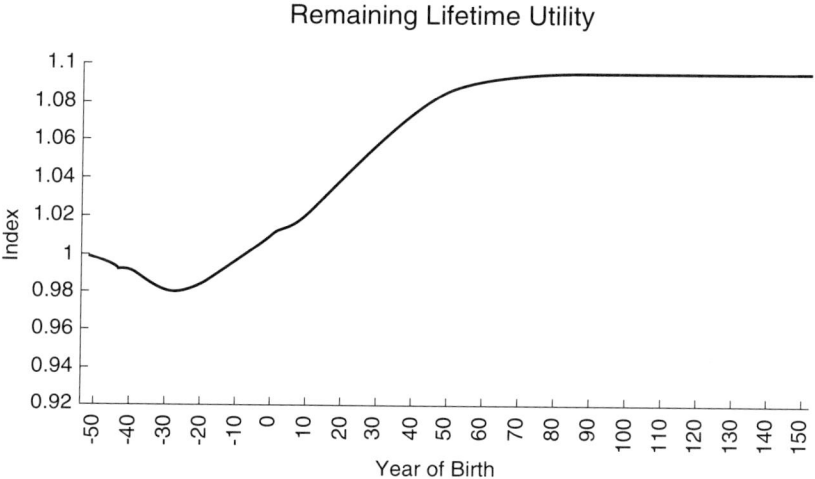

FIGURE 1. *Proportional income tax financing of benefits.*

tion's remaining lifetime utility under privatization is 6 percent higher than it would have been in the initial steady state. To be precise, the percent change in utility is measured as a wealth equivalent, specifically, as the percent change in initial steady-state remaining lifetime resources needed to achieve the level of utility experienced as a result of privatizing social security.

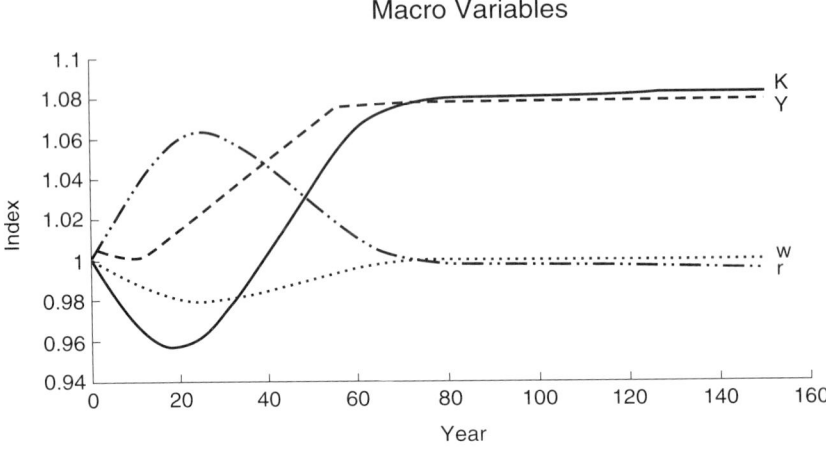

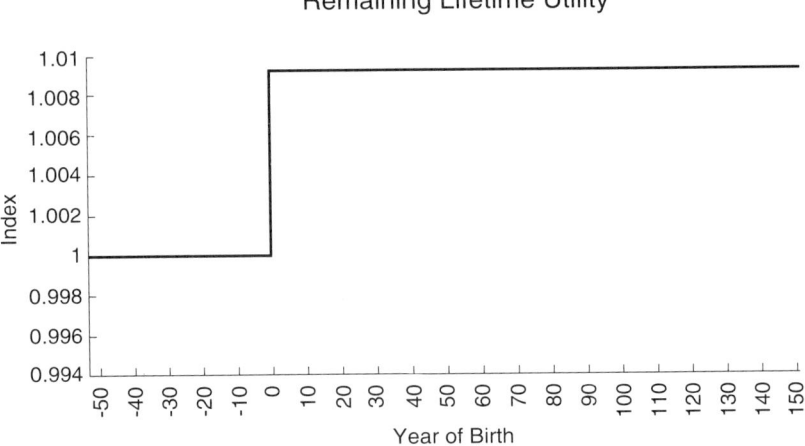

FIGURE 2. *Proportional income tax financing of benefits: welfare of living generations constant.*

As Figure 1 shows, privatizing social security in the base-case manner is highly beneficial to the economy over the long run. Compared with the initial steady state, the long-run capital stock, output, and wage are 52.2, 15.9, and 9.5 percent larger, respectively. The long-run interest rate is 23.9 percent smaller. The income tax rate, which was 20.0 percent in the initial steady state, rises immediately to 28.8 percent but declines

TABLE 1
Percent Change in Capital Stock Relative to Steady State

Tax financing govt. spending	Tax financing soc. sec. benefits	LSRA	TBL	Deficits for first 5 years	Year of transition			
					5	10	25	150
Yprop	Yprop	No	No	No	−0.32	−0.02	6.59	52.19
Yprop	Yprop	Yes	No	No	−1.54	−3.11	−3.71	8.46
Yprop	Yprop	No	Yes	No	−2.89	−4.92	−0.90	43.18
Yprop	Yprop	Yes	Yes	No	−5.21	−10.43	−16.83	−8.88
Yprop	Yprop	No	No	Yes	2.93	−0.32	−2.86	35.40
Yprop	C	Yes	No	No	1.91	3.92	8.65	12.92
Yprog	C	No	No	No	5.54	11.54	25.60	56.67
Yprog	C	Yes	No	No	3.13	6.51	14.07	21.44

govt., government; soc. sec., social security; LSRA, lump sum redistribution authority; TBL, tax–benefit linkage; Yprop, proportional income tax; Yprog, progressive income tax; C, proportional consumption tax.

TABLE 2
Percent Change in Output Relative to Steady State

Tax financing govt. spending	Tax financing soc. sec. benefits	LSRA	TBL	Deficits for first 5 years	Year of transition			
					5	10	25	150
Yprop	Yprop	No	No	No	0.96	1.19	5.02	15.86
Yprop	Yprop	Yes	No	No	0.30	0.11	2.37	8.07
Yprop	Yprop	No	Yes	No	−5.98	−6.05	−2.41	8.08
Yprop	Yprop	Yes	Yes	No	−7.14	−7.85	−6.36	−1.34
Yprop	Yprop	No	No	Yes	6.67	−1.33	0.90	11.81
Yprop	C	Yes	No	No	2.78	3.18	5.38	8.92
Yprog	C	No	No	No	5.23	6.20	9.79	17.11
Yprog	C	Yes	No	No	4.21	4.80	7.25	11.05

govt., government; soc. sec., social security; LSRA, lump sum redistribution authority; TBL, tax–benefit linkage; Yprop, proportional income tax; Yprog, progressive income tax; C, proportional consumption tax.

over time, ultimately ending up lower than it started, at a value of 17.3 percent.

The message of Figure 2 is that almost all of the long-run economic gains in Figure 1 from privatizing social security are due to the policy's redistribution from initial generations to future ones. When compensation is provided to initial generations, the long-run gain in utility is not

TABLE 3
Percent Change in Wage Relative to Steady State

Tax financing govt. spending	Tax financing soc. soc. benefits	LSRA	TBL	Deficits for first 5 years	Year of transition			
					5	10	25	150
Yprop	Yprop	No	No	No	−0.43	−0.40	0.50	9.52
Yprop	Yprop	Yes	No	No	−0.62	−1.08	−2.02	0.12
Yprop	Yprop	No	Yes	No	1.08	0.40	0.51	9.83
Yprop	Yprop	Yes	Yes	No	0.69	−0.94	−3.88	−2.61
Yprop	Yprop	No	No	Yes	−1.18	0.50	−1.26	6.59
Yprop	C	Yes	No	No	−0.28	0.24	1.02	1.20
Yprog	C	No	No	No	−0.25	1.65	4.59	10.19
Yprog	C	Yes	No	No	−0.35	0.54	2.08	3.02

govt., government; soc. sec., social security; LSRA, lump sum redistribution authority; TBL, tax–benefit linkage; Yprop, proportional income tax; Yprog, progressive income tax; C, proportional consumption tax.

TABLE 4
Percentage Change in Interest Rate Relative to Steady State

Tax financing govt. spending	Tax financing soc. sec. benefits	LSRA	TBL	Deficits for first 5 years	Year of Transition			
					5	10	25	150
Yprop	Yprop	No	No	No	1.29	1.20	−1.48	−23.87
Yprop	Yprop	Yes	No	No	1.87	3.33	6.32	−0.36
Yprop	Yprop	No	Yes	No	−3.17	−1.19	−1.50	−24.50
Yprop	Yprop	Yes	Yes	No	−2.05	2.88	12.59	8.26
Yprop	Yprop	No	No	Yes	3.64	−1.65	3.87	−17.42
Yprop	C	Yes	No	No	0.85	−0.71	−3.00	−3.55
Yprog	C	No	No	No	−2.22	−4.78	−12.59	−25.25
Yprog	C	Yes	No	No	1.04	−1.60	−5.98	−8.55

govt., government; soc. sec., social security; LSRA, lump sum redistribution authority; TBL, tax–benefit linkage; Yprop, proportional income tax; Yprog, progressive income tax; C, proportional consumption tax.

9.7 percent, but only 0.9 percent. In addition, the respective long-run increases in the capital stock, output, and wage are 8.5, 8.1, and 0.1 percent, respectively, much smaller than the corresponding 52.2, 15.9, and 9.5 percent increases shown in Figure 1. Although the efficiency gain is small compared with the long-run utility gain in Figure 1, it is certainly not trivial. Nor is it small compared with the efficiency gains

TABLE 5
Percent Change in Remaining Lifetime Utility

Tax financing govt. spending	Tax financing soc. sec. benefits	LSRA	TBL	Deficits for first 5 years	Year of birth						
					−54	−25	−10	0	10	25	150
Yprop	Yprop	No	No	No	−0.12	−1.84	−0.17	1.19	2.38	5.17	9.67
Yprop	Yprop	Yes	No	No	0	0	0	0.93	0.93	0.93	0.93
Yprop	Yprop	No	Yes	No	−0.24	−3.06	−1.26	0.31	1.39	4.29	8.89
Yprop	Yprop	Yes	Yes	No	0	0	0	−3.14	−3.14	−3.14	−3.14
Yprop	Yprop	No	No	Yes	0.09	−0.90	0.12	0.99	0.13	2.55	7.43
Yprop	C	Yes	No	No	0	0	0	2.09	2.09	2.09	2.09
Yprog	C	No	No	No	−4.71	−1.19	1.81	3.55	5.07	7.57	10.79
Yprog	C	Yes	No	No	0	0	0	4.45	4.45	4.45	4.45

govt., government; soc. sec., social security; LSRA, lump sum redistribution authority; TBL, tax–benefit linkage; Yprop, proportional income tax; Yprog, progressive income tax; C, proportional consumption tax.

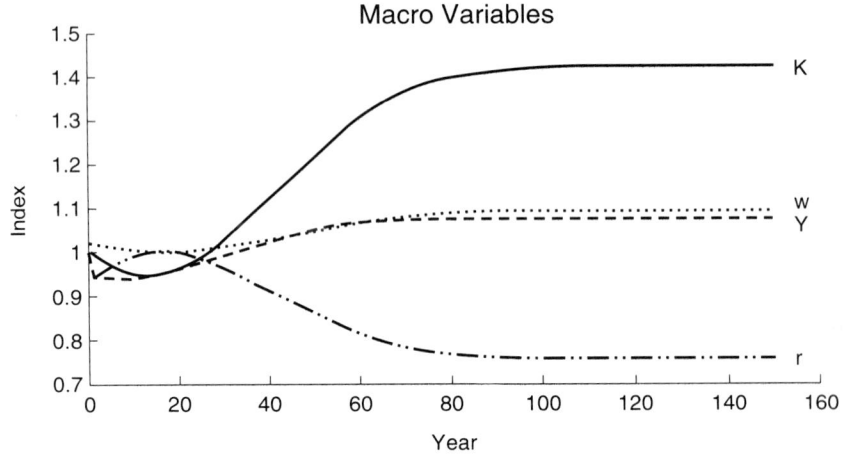

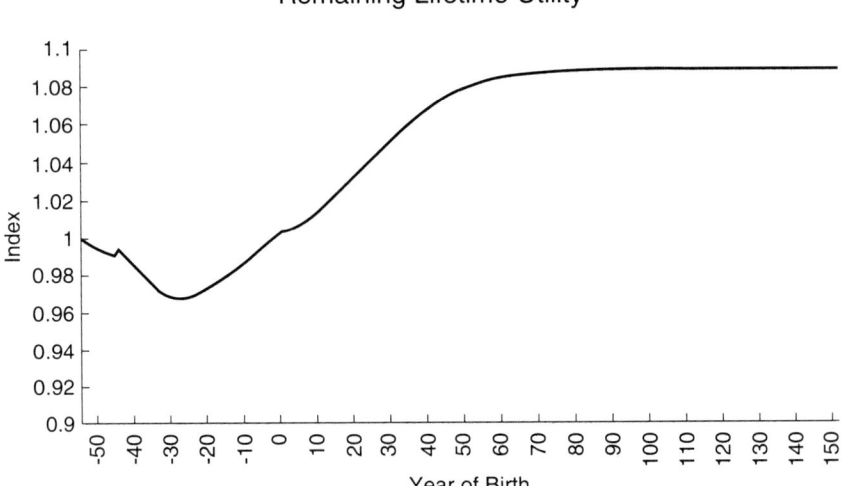

FIGURE 3. *Proportional income tax financing of benefits: perfect tax–benefit linkage.*

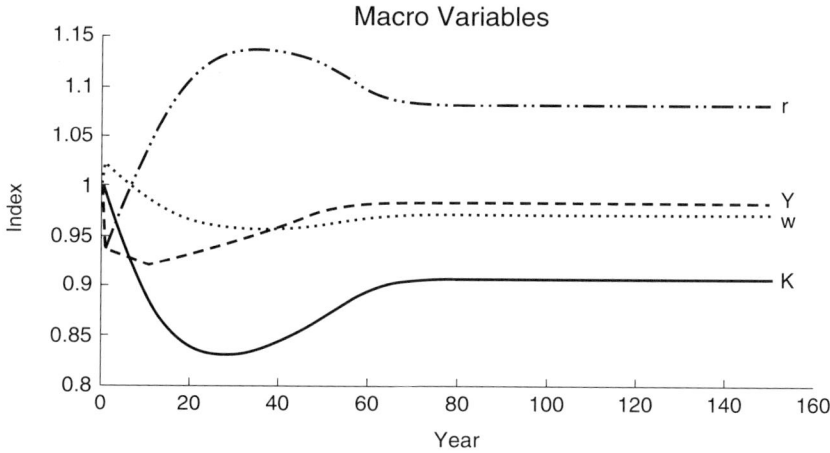

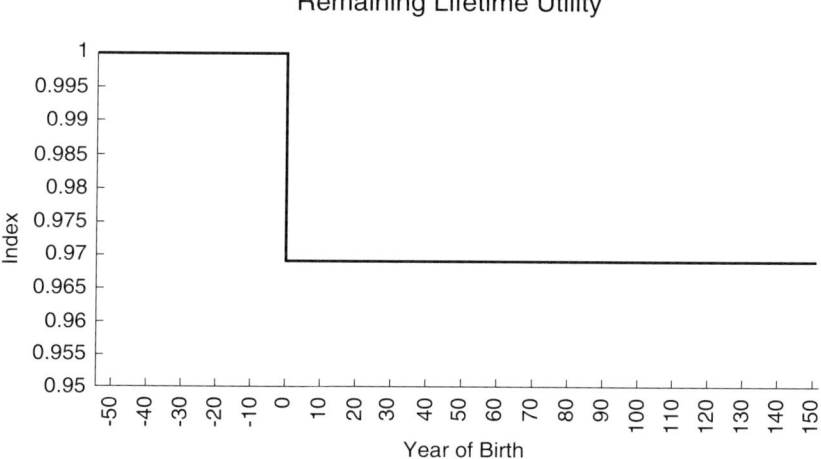

FIGURE 4. *Proportional income tax financing of benefits: perfect tax–benefit linkage and welfare of living generations constant.*

available from other fiscal reforms, such as switching from income to consumption taxation.

What is the source of the efficiency gain? Is it related to the fact that in the base-case steady state, the pay-as-you-go social security system features zero marginal benefit–tax linkage? Figures 3 and 4 answer this question. They repeat the simulations of Figures 1 and 2 but starting from a steady state in which each dollar contributed to social security is viewed as providing future benefits with the present value of $1.[6] Figure 3, like Figure 1, shows that absent the LSRA's compensation of initial generations, privatization has very significant positive long-run effects on the economy. But as Figure 4 makes clear, once one compensates initial generations, future generations actually end up worse off; that is, Figure 4 indicates that privatizing from a situation of full benefit–tax linkage is inefficient. Indeed, keeping all initial generations at their preprivatization level of utility and producing a uniform level of utility for future generations (those born after the reform) entails a quite substantial 3.1 percent reduction in the utility levels of these future generations. Interestingly, the long-run values of the capital stock, output, and real wage are all smaller as a result of privatizing social security coupled with the LSRA compensation policy.

Intuitively, privatization adds, at least temporarily, an additional distortion to the fiscal structure, namely that arising from the use of general revenue finance—in this case, income taxation—to finance benefits during the benefit phaseout period. The temporarily higher income tax rates distort both labor supply and intertemporal consumption decisions. Given this fact, the only way that privatization can improve economic efficiency is if the temporary income tax distortion replaces a permanent social security tax distortion. But since privatization in Figure 4 phases out a nondistortionary social security system, it must be inefficient.

3.5 Using Debt Finance During the Privatization Transition

An alternative to raising income tax rates immediately is to borrow. Figure 5 considers a simulation in which the government borrows to meet all social security benefits for the first 5 years of privatization. Thereafter, the government raises the income tax rate to maintain a constant ratio of debt per capita. Note that this policy features short-run crowding-out but long-run crowding-in of the capital stock. The 5-year borrowing policy mitigates much of the utility losses to initial generations, leaving future generations with a 7 percent higher level of welfare. Waiting for 10 years to stabilize the debt goes too far in helping initial generations and, consequently, ends up making certain future generations significantly worse off. For example, the generation born 8 years after the reform suffers a 3 percent utility loss from the policy. The moral here is that short-term deficit finance can help protect initial generations from adverse effects of privatization, but it is easy to go overboard.

[6] Again, we know that pay-as-you-go social security cannot on average and in the long run pay benefits whose present values equal tax contributions, assuming as we do that the marginal product of capital exceeds the economy's growth rate. But this does not preclude social security's paying, at the margin, a present dollar in benefits for each dollar contributed.

Macro Variables

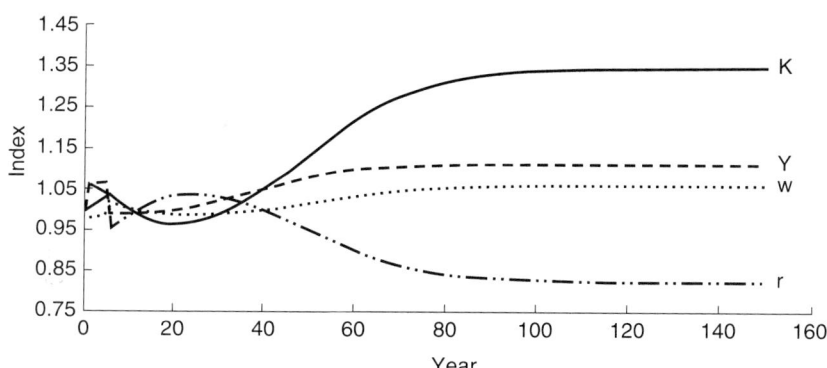

Remaining Lifetime Utility

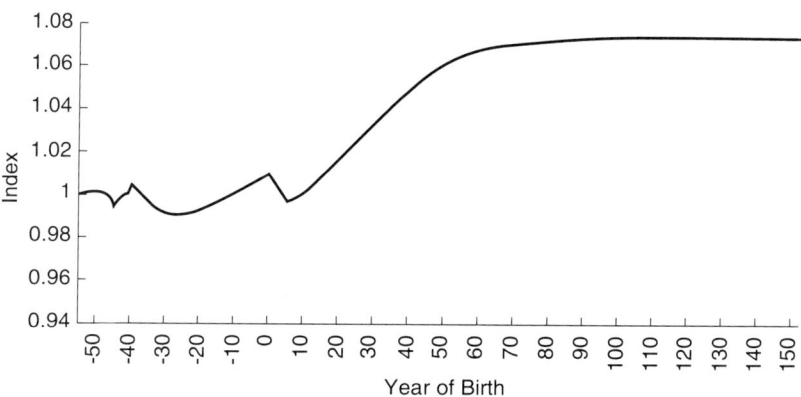

FIGURE 5. *Proportional income tax financing of benefits: 5-year debt finance.*

3.6 Using Consumption Taxes to Finance Benefits During the Transition

Figure 6 shows that the choice of tax base used to finance social security benefits during the transition can alter macro-outcomes and the efficiency gains from reform. Figure 6 repeats the LSRA privatization experiment of

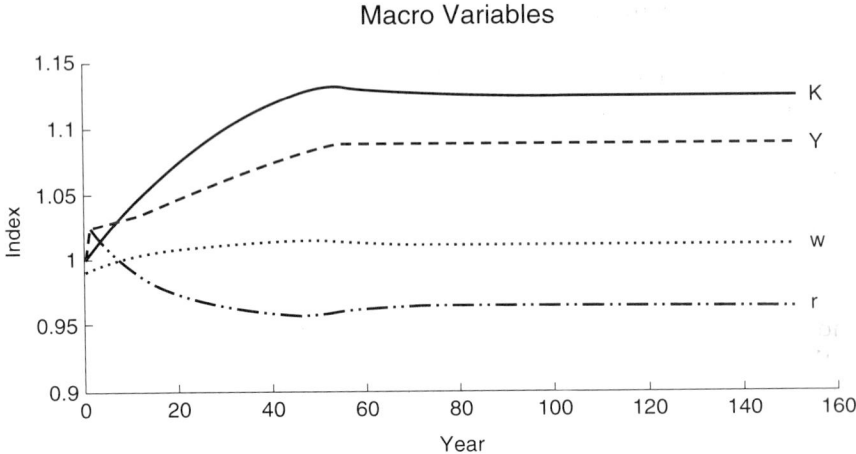

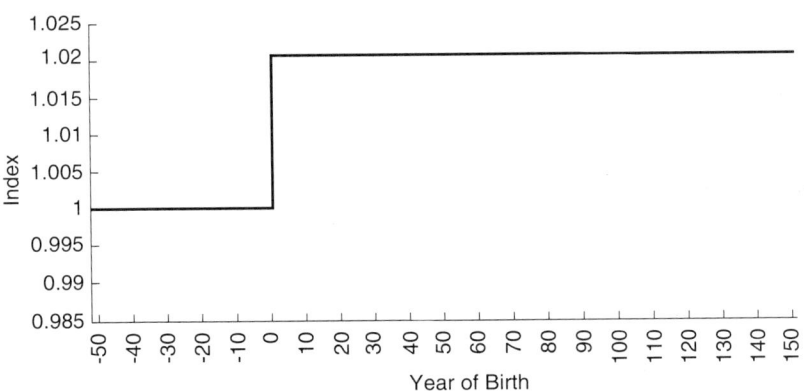

FIGURE 6. *Proportional consumption tax financing of benefits: proportional income tax financing of general revenues and welfare of living generations constant.*

Figure 2 with one exception. It uses consumption taxation to pay for social security benefits during the phaseout of those benefits. Using consumption taxes to finance social security benefits leads to more crowding in of the capital stock. The intuition for this result is that in using consumption taxation to help finance the transition, a larger burden of paying for remaining social security benefits is shifted onto older generations who have a larger propensity to consume. Figure 6 also shows a larger efficiency gain than does Figure 2. Future generations are made better off by 2.1 percent rather than by 0.9 percent. This is what one would expect given that consumption taxation is more efficient than income taxation. As discussed in Auerbach and Kotlikoff (1987), consumption taxation is significantly more efficient than income taxation because it embeds a one-time nondistortionary wealth tax. In the simulation under consideration, the consumption tax is also used only temporarily—until all benefits are phased out—and during the phaseout period, the consumption tax rate steadily declines. The temporary nature of the consumption tax and the fact that its rate falls over time may also improve economic efficiency. The reason is that it provides the model's households with an incentive to delay consuming until the consumption tax rate is reduced. This incentive to delay consuming somewhat offsets the incentive to consume earlier rather than later, arising from the capital income tax component of the income tax.

3.7 Privatizing Starting with Progressive Income or Proportional Consumption Taxation

The privatization of social security can also start from steady states featuring other than a proportional income tax regime. If, for example, one starts with a progressive income tax, with an average marginal rate of 32.9 percent, and adjusts all marginal tax rates during the transition by the same percentage, one ends up with results similar to those depicted in Figures 1 and 2. The same is true if one starts with a proportional consumption tax and adjusts the consumption tax rate over the transition to cover remaining social security benefits.

The simulations underlying Figures 7 and 8 also start with a progressive income tax but use a consumption tax to finance transitional benefits. Figure 8 indicates much greater potential efficiency gains than does Figure 6. In this case, the efficiency gain is a substantial 4.5 percent. As with the comparison between Figures 2 and 4, the size of the gain in Figure 8 depends critically on the assumption of a zero social security benefit–tax linkage. Rerunning the Figure 8 simulation under the assumption of a full benefit–tax linkage produces an efficiency loss of 3.2 percent!

4. PRIVATIZING SOCIAL SECURITY IN THE UNITED STATES: AN EXAMPLE

In the Fall 1994 final report of the Entitlements Commission, Senators Danforth and Kerry proposed a limited privatization of social security.

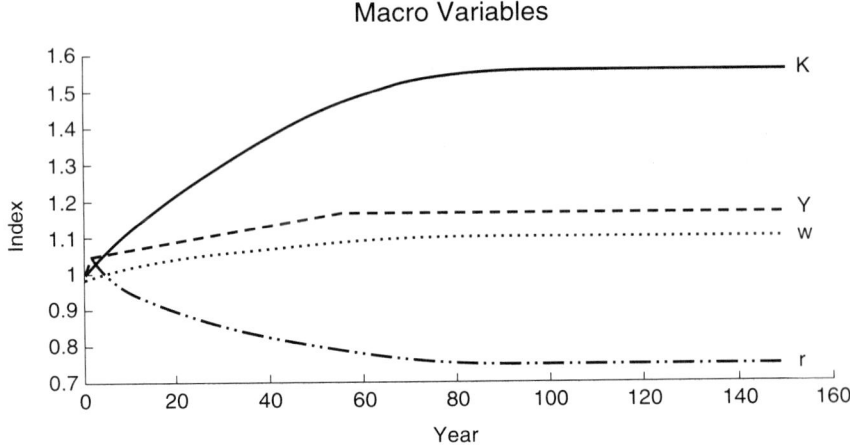

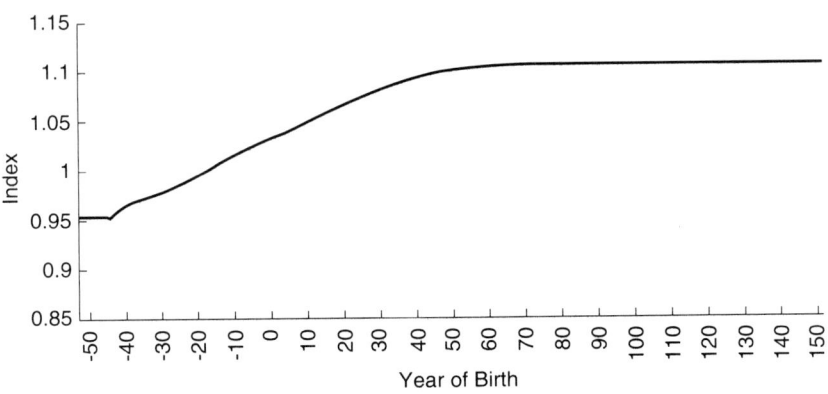

FIGURE 7. *Proportional consumption tax financing of benefits: progressive income tax financing of general revenues.*

Their scheme involves using 1.5 percentage points of each worker's social security payroll tax contribution to fund a personal retirement account for the worker. The proposal applies to all workers 50 years old and under. Like 401(k) and Keogh plans, workers would control the investment of moneys in their accounts. Earnings on the accounts would be taxable when funds were withdrawn. Withdrawals would be permitted only in

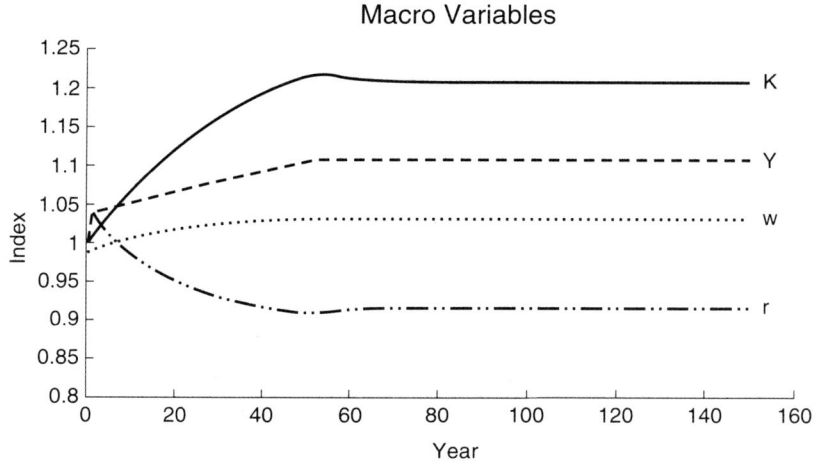

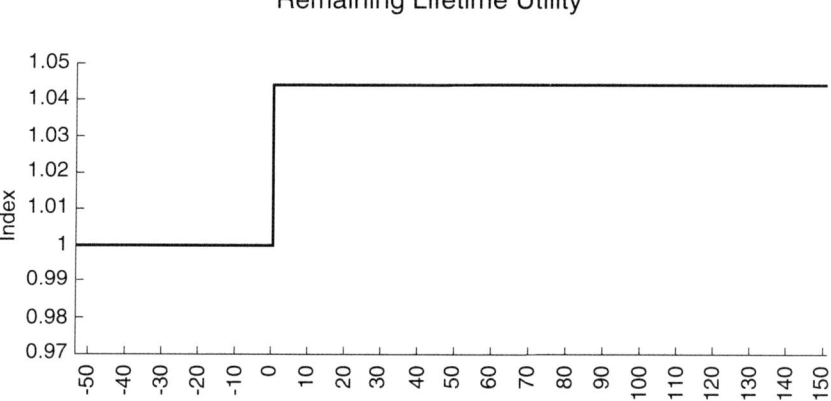

FIGURE 8. *Proportional consumption tax financing of benefits: progressive income tax financing of general revenues and welfare of living generations constant.*

the case of disability or retirement. Unlike 401(k) and Keogh plans, contributions would not be deductible. The Danforth–Kerry social security privatization proposal leaves social security benefits unchanged, although other proposals in their report reduce these benefits.

Since the combined employer–employee Old Age, Survivor, and Disability Insurance (OASDI) payroll tax rate exceeds 12 percent, the Danforth–Kerry proposal envisions privatizing only about one eighth of current social security taxes and zero percent of social security benefits. As such, the proposal's goals are rather modest. Indeed, the most significant feature of the Danforth–Kerry proposal is not in its details, but in the fact that prominent members of Congress are now taking privatizing social security seriously. This fact opens the door for a broad public debate about the merits and demerits of the System and how it might best be privatized.

4.1 Illustration of Social Security Privatization

In offering such a modest proposal and one that left social security benefits unchanged, Senators Danforth and Kerry avoided the potentially tricky issue of how to credit past contributions and how to privatize survivor and disability insurance benefits. This section illustrates a simple method for privatizing social security—the Personal Security System—that deals with these issues.[7] The objective here is not to advocate privatizing social security but simply to illustrate that certain types of privatization are easily accomplished. Having an explicit proposal to consider also helps focus attention on particular issues that arise in considering privatization.

4.2 The Personal Security System

The Personal Security System is a straightforward method of crediting past contributions and uses social security's own benefit schedule. It also separates the survivor and disability insurance programs from the Old Age Insurance (OAI) part of social security and leaves them within social security. The Personal Security System privatizes the total (employer plus employee) contribution to OAI by investing it in personal retirement accounts (PRAs) for all workers below age 62. The OAI component of total OASDI contributions refers here to the ratio of social security retirement benefits to total OASDI benefits. This ratio would remain fixed through time at its current value of 0.68. Hence, 68 percent of current and future projected total contributions to social security would be allocated to the funding of PRAs.

The OAI contribution for married workers would be divided into equal shares and invested in two PRAs, one for each spouse. Withdrawals from PRAs would be permitted only in the event of disability or the

---

[7] A version of this social security privatization proposal was developed as part of a Data Resources, Inc. project on which I worked with Dr. Cynthia Latta of Data Resources, Inc.

attainment of age 62, which is the youngest age at which social security retirement benefits can now be received. Contributions to PRAs would not be subject to federal income taxes, thus maintaining the current federal income tax treatment of employer contributions. Withdrawals from PRAs would be subject to federal income taxation. Hence, PRAs would receive the same tax and regulatory treatment as current 401(k) and Keogh plans. Indeed, employers with existing 401(k) plans could make PRA contributions on behalf of their employees to those accounts as well as to new 401(k) accounts that they would establish for the spouses of their workers. Self-employed workers with Keogh accounts could make their PRA contributions to their existing Keogh accounts as well as to new accounts that they would establish for their spouses. The PRAs would afford the same protection to surviving spouses in the event of the death of the account owner as is provided with respect to current 401(k) and Keogh accounts.

Employers as well as employees would still contribute to social security for survivor and disability insurance. The proposal leaves social security survivor and disability benefits unchanged; that is, these benefits continue to be calculated on the basis of workers' social security-covered earnings histories.

Each worker under age 62 at the time of the reform would receive social security retirement (OAI) benefits to the extent that he or she had contributed to the system before the reform. The benefit would still be calculated using social security's benefit formula, but the earnings record used in the calculation would have entries of zero for years after the reform was initiated.[8]

For example, the average monthly earnings of a worker who is 35 at the time of the reform and began covered employment at age 25 will be based on his or her covered earnings between ages 25 and 35, with the worker's covered earnings record after age 35 filled in with zeros. Dependent OAI benefits for spouses of retired workers would continue to be based on the retired worker's postreform social security retirement benefit.

4.3 *Financing the Transition*

The reform would obviously reduce contributions to the Social Security System that are now being used to make current benefit payments and to build up a significant reserve in the Social Security Trust Fund. This

---

[8] Gustman and Steinmeier (1995) propose an alternative method of calculating benefits during the transition to a fully privatized social security system. Their method provides workers with a benefit equal to the social security benefit they would otherwise receive, multiplied by the fraction of benefit computation years the worker spent participating under the current system.

shortfall in revenues would be borrowed by the Treasury. Interest payments on this borrowing would be paid through general revenue finance. Although the government's explicit debt would increase as a result of the reform, its implicit social security liability would decline. As previously described, the macroeconomic impact of the proposal would depend on the type of general revenue finance used to pay for interest on the additional explicit debt issued during the transition.

4.4 Discussion

This proposal leaves social security survivor and disability benefits unchanged. In so doing, it avoids the highly complex problem of determining the amounts of life and disability insurance that different households with very different ages, incomes, health status, and other characteristics should be forced to purchase from the private market. It also avoids having to confront issues of adverse selection and moral hazard that plague private market provision of insurance, particularly disability insurance.

The proposal would be easy to implement. It piggybacks on existing 401(k) and Keogh regulation, thereby avoiding the need for new regulations covering PRAs. In addition, the Social Security Administration can modify its calculation of benefits for those participating in the Personal Security System by simply changing a few lines of computer code in the software that it currently uses to compute benefits.

The proposal's phasing out of social security retirement and dependent benefits based on past contributions is gradual. Consequently, there will be no "notch-baby" problems in which one age group can claim to be treated unfairly relative to generations either slightly younger or older. The benefit phaseout uses social security's own mechanism for adjusting benefits for shorter work histories. As a result, the phaseout of benefits is likely to be viewed as fair.

Employers' contributions to PRAs are shared equally between the husband and wife. This "earnings sharing" guarantees that nonworking spouses will have retirement income even in the case of divorce. In contrast, the current social security system guarantees OAI dependent benefits for nonworking divorced spouses only if they were married for 10 years before becoming divorced. The proposal also enhances overall survivor protection for spouses. It does so by leaving survivor insurance benefits unchanged but providing, in accordance with 401(k) and Keogh regulations, surviving spouses with a first claim on the PRAs of their decedent husband or wife. In addition, the proposal's earnings sharing reduces the substantial and capricious redistribution from two-earner couples and single individuals to one-earner couples that occurs under the current system (see Boskin et al., 1987; Steurle and Bakija, 1994).

The proposal provides for individual ownership and investment control of PRA accounts. As a result, workers would most likely view their PRA contributions as equivalent to private saving, which would strengthen the linkage between old-age income and contributions.

Since social security uses a highly progressive benefit schedule based on lifetime earnings, one might question whether the Personal Security System would be as progressive as the existing system. It might, for two reasons. First, unlike social security benefits whose federal income taxation is limited, *all* moneys withdrawn from PRAs would be taxed under the progressive federal income tax. Second, social security benefits are provided in the form of annuities, so those who live longer receive more benefits than those who do not. Since the poor, on average, die at a much younger age than the rich, providing benefits in the form of annuities can be quite regressive (Rogot, Sorlie, and Johnson 1992). Indeed, depending on the rate at which one discounts social security benefits and taxes, social security's regressivity due to longevity differences between the rich and poor can fully offset the progressivity resulting from its benefit formula. These points notwithstanding, the government could easily modify the proposed Personal Security System to make it more progressive by matching individual contributions at a rate that declined with the size of the contribution.

In contrast to social security's annuitized benefits, PRAs would represent a form of net worth. Although households would be free to purchase annuities after age 62 with their PRA accounts, they would not be compelled to do so. Most would probably not annuitize their PRA assets. Why? Because the private annuities market suffers from the same problem of adverse selection as do other insurance markets. In this case, individuals with a longer than average life expectancy are most eager to purchase annuities. Their participation in the market pushes up the price of annuities for those with a normal expected life span (see Friedman and Warshawsky, 1990).[9]

Although reducing social security's annuitization of the poor will redistribute to them, the reduced annuitization of their old-age resources will leave the poor as well as the rich exposed to more longevity risk. Note that longevity risk can be of substantial economic importance (Kotlikoff

---

[9] There is of course a significant private market in employer-provided defined benefit pensions. By pooling together the longevity risks of large numbers of workers who did not select their employment on the basis of their longevity, employers are able to overcome the adverse selection that plagues the market in individual annuities.

and Spivak, 1981). Although reducing the availability of insurance of any kind, including annuity insurance, is economically inefficient, it would most likely raise our rate of national saving by prompting the elderly to consume less in old age and leave larger unintended bequests (see Auerbach, Kotlikoff, and Weil, 1992, and Auerbach et al., 1995).

Another issue is whether some members of the public would invest their PRA contributions unwisely. Wise investors understand the benefits of a diversified portfolio that includes holding a significant share of one's assets in foreign as well as domestic equities. Given the propensity of many defined contribution plan participants to avoid equities and other assets perceived to be "risky," it is clear that a significant financial educational program would most likely be needed to assist the public in choosing its investment strategies. If improved financial education did not succeed in getting the general public to choose well-balanced portfolios, then the government might limit the choice of investments in the PRA to a single world index fund.

The Personal Security System or similar schemes are likely to entail higher administration costs. Diamond and Valdes-Prieto (1994) report that administration costs of U.S. defined contribution plans are several times higher than those of the Social Security Administration when scaled by the number of participants. Since the Personal Security System proposal leaves social security's administrative responsibilities essentially unchanged, at least for quite some time, the proposal entails higher administrative costs.

A final issue is intergenerational risk sharing. As Merton (1983) shows, pay-as-you-go social security, in combination with other fiscal policies, can be used to pool labor and capital income risks between the young and the old. Pay-as-you-go social security can also be used to pool risk between current and future generations. However, since other fiscal instruments will still be available, such as conventional deficit finance or changes in the tax structure that redistributes across generations, the government's capacity for intergenerational risk sharing is not likely to be greatly affected by the adoption of this proposal.

5. CONCLUSION

The privatizing of social security is spreading from South America. It could well spread to the United States as politicians grapple with ways of addressing the fiscal/demographic debacle facing the country. This paper's simulations of the AK model show that privatizing social security is likely to generate major long-run increases in output and living standards. But unless privatization includes compensation to initial generations, these long-run gains will come primarily at their expense. This said, the pure efficiency gains from privatization can be substantial. Their precise size depends on the existing tax structure, the linkage between benefits and taxes under the existing social security system, and the choice of the tax instrument used to finance benefits during the transition. When the initial tax structure features a progressive income tax, when benefit–tax linkage is low, when consumption taxation is used to finance social security benefits during the transition, and when existing generations are fully compensated for their privatization losses, there is a 4.5 percent welfare gain to future generations. But if these circumstances do not hold, the efficiency gains from privatization are likely to be smaller, possibly even negative.

The illustrative Personal Security System shows that there are simple ways to privatize the retirement portion of the U.S. Social Security System and to credit workers for their past social security contributions. It also suggests that privatizing social security could provide more survivor protection than the current system as well as eliminate much of the current system's seemingly capricious redistribution between two-earner and single-earner couples. But the proposal's analysis also suggests that these benefits from privatization must be set against a possible reduction in progressivity and a likely reduction in the amount of longevity insurance available to the elderly through annuities.

REFERENCES

Arrau, Patricio (1990). "Social Security Reform: The Capital Accumulation and Intergenerational Distribution Effect." Washington, DC: World Bank.
———, and Klaus Schmidt-Hebbel (1993). "Macroeconomic and Intergenerational Welfare Effects of a Transition from Pay-as-You-Go to Fully Funded Pensions." Washington, DC: World Bank, Policy Research Department, Macroeconomics and Growth Division.
Auerbach, Alan J., and Laurence J. Kotlikoff (1987). *Dynamic Fiscal Policy*. Cambridge, England: Cambridge University Press.
———, Laurence J. Kotlikoff, and David N. Weil (1992). "The Increasing Annuitization of the Elderly." NBER Working Paper no. 4182, October.
———, Jagadeesh Gokhale, Laurence Kotlikoff, John Sabelhaus, and David N. Weil (1995). "The Annuitization of Americans' Resources: A Cohort Analysis." NBER Working Paper no. 5089, April.
Boskin, Michael J., Laurence J. Kotlikoff, Douglas J. Puffert, and John B. Shoven (1987). "Social Security: A Financial Appraisal Across and Within Generations." *National Tax Journal* 40(no. 1, March):19–34.
Diamond, Peter, and Salvador Valdes-Prieto (1994). "Social Security Reform." In *The Chilean Economy: Policy Lessons and Challenges*, Barry Bosworth, Rudiger Dornbusch, and Raul Laben (eds.). Washington, DC: The Brookings Institution.

Feldstein, Martin (1995). "Would Privatizing Social Security Raise Economic Welfare?" Boston: Harvard University, August. Mimeographed.
Friedman, Benjamin, and Mark Wahrshawsky (1990). "The Cost of Annuities: Implications for Saving and Behavior." *The Quarterly Journal of Economics* CV(no. 1, February):135–154.
Gokhale, Jagadeesh, Laurence J. Kotlikoff, and John Sabelhaus (1996). "Understanding the Postwar Decline in U.S. Saving: A Cohort Analysis." Forthcoming in *The Brookings Papers on Economic Activity*.
Gustman, Alan L., and Thomas L. Steinmeier (1995). "Privatizing Social Security." September. Mimeo, Department of Economics, Dartmouth College.
Imrohoroglu, Selahattin, He Huang, and Thomas J. Sargent (1995). "Two Computational Experiments to Privatize Social Security." University of Southern California, March. Mimeographed.
Kotlikoff, Laurence J. (1992). *Generational Accounting*. New York: The Free Press.
———, and Avia Spivak. (1981). "The Family as an Incomplete Annuities Market." *Journal of Political Economy* 89(no. 2, April): 372–391.
Merton, Robert C. (1983). "On the Role of Social Security as a Means for Efficient Risk Sharing in an Economy Where Human Capital Is Not Tradable." In *Financial Aspects of the U.S. Pension System*. Zvi Bodie and John B. Shoven (eds.). Chicago: University of Chicago Press, pp. 325–358.
Raffelhueschen, Bernd (1993). "Funding Social Security Through Pareto-Optimal Conversion Policies." *Journal of Economics/Zeitschrift für Nationalökonomie*. Supplement 7:105–131.
Rogot, Eugene, Paul D. Sorlie, and Norman J. Johnson (1992). "Life Expectancy by Employment Status, Income and Education in the National Longitudinal Mortality Study." *Public Health Reports* 107(no. 4, July/August):457–461.
Steurle, C. Eugene, and Jon M. Bakija (1994). *Retooling Social Security for the 21st Century*. Washington, DC: The Urban Institute Press.
World Bank (1994). *Averting The Old Age Crisis*. Oxford, England: Oxford University Press.

WHY HAVE SEPARATE ENVIRONMENTAL TAXES?

Don Fullerton
University of Texas at Austin

EXECUTIVE SUMMARY

Each environmental tax in the United States is designed to collect revenue for a trust fund used to clean up a particular pollution problem. Each might be intended to collect from a particular industry thought to be responsible for that pollution problem, but none represents a good example of an incentive-based tax designed to discourage the polluting activity itself.

A different tax for each trust fund means that each tax rate is typically less than 1 percent. But each separate tax has an extra cost of administration and compliance, since taxpayers must read another set of rules and fill out another set of forms. This paper provides evidence on compliance costs that are high relative to the small revenue from each separate tax. In addition, an input–output model is used to show how current U.S. environmental tax burdens are passed from taxed industries to all other industries. Thus, the extra cost incurred to administer each separate tax achieves neither targeted incentives nor targeted burdens.

This paper was prepared for presentation at the National Bureau of Economic Research Conference on Tax Policy and the Economy, Washington, D.C., November 7, 1995. I am grateful for excellent research assistance from Patricia Saydah, financial assistance from the NBER and National Science Foundation grant SBR-9413334, and helpful suggestions from Tom Barthold, Bruce Davie, Virginia McConnell, Peter Merrill, Jim Poterba, Seng-su Tsang, Margaret Walls, and Randy Weiss. This paper is part of the NBER Research Program in Public Economics. Any opinions expressed are those of the author and not those of the National Science Foundation or the NBER.

1. INTRODUCTION

Many economists and policymakers are beginning to discuss potential gains from better coordination of environmental policy and tax policy. If properly designed, certain taxes can help prevent environmental harm while raising revenue that can be used to reduce other distorting taxes or to feed a trust fund for the cleanup of existing environmental problems. Yet the design of such taxes is difficult. Even without coordination, environmental policy and tax policy must each strike a balance among competing economic and political objectives. With attempts to coordinate these policies, the trade-offs become all the more complicated.

This paper is concerned with the design of taxes that might coordinate environmental and tax policies and with the trade-off among three particular objectives. First, a tax might be designed to discourage an activity that causes environmental harm. A tax on vehicle emissions, for example, would provide incentives to reduce emissions by fixing the vehicle's pollution control equipment, scrapping old vehicles, driving less aggressively, or reducing total mileage.

Second, a tax might be designed to place its burden on those responsible for a particular environmental problem. This objective relates to fairness rather than incentives. The tax on vehicle emissions would meet both objectives because it would discourage the polluting activity while collecting from those responsible. But environmental taxes do not necessarily meet both objectives. The emissions tax may soon be feasible, but it is not yet in place. Meanwhile, the United States relies on a combination of other policies, including a tax on gasoline. This tax does collect from those who drive vehicles and are thus responsible for the pollution, but it does not provide incentives to fix pollution control equipment or otherwise reduce emissions per mile driven.

Third, a tax might be designed to minimize administrative cost to the government and compliance cost imposed on taxpayers. The same example highlights the trade-off among these objectives: a tax on vehicle emissions might have better incentives to reduce emissions, but it would be difficult and therefore costly to administer. The gasoline tax might provide the best balance among objectives: since it has some of the desired incentives to reduce driving, it places its burden on those who emit pollutants, and it is easily collected.

In discussing these three objectives, this paper abstracts from many other interesting problems and objectives of policy. Also, the paper does not attempt a comprehensive evaluation of all U.S. environmental taxes. Any tax may have environmental effects, and none can be evaluated fully in this limited space. Instead, the paper uses selected examples of the trade-offs among these three objectives. Section 2 discusses the design of environmental taxes generally, including the trade-off among many possible objectives. Section 3 provides evidence on administrative costs and estimates some compliance costs. Section 4 reviews the effects of some actual U.S. environmental taxes, and Section 5 presents a case study of an incentive-based tax that failed. Finally, Section 6 presents an input–output model and uses it to estimate the shifting of U.S. environmental tax burdens from taxed industries to other industries.

Any generalization might be considered adventurous, since each U.S. tax has somewhat different effects on incentives, burdens, and compliance costs. Nevertheless, three conclusions emerge from this analysis. First, in general, U.S. policy has not used "environmental taxes" for incentives to discourage pollution. The United States has no tax on vehicle emissions, no tax on smokestack emissions, and no tax on the generation or disposal of waste. Instead, actual policy has put great weight on the second objective—to collect from those responsible for pollution. Congress seems concerned not with incentives for future behavior, but with funding the cleaning up of past pollution at existing toxic waste sites, oil spills, and leaky underground storage tanks. The U.S. imposes "environmental" taxes on chemicals, petroleum, and other inputs to production. These taxes may collect from the industries responsible for contaminated sites, and they finance various trust funds for the cleanup of those sites, but they do not discourage behavior that leads to contamination or spills. To put the point more strongly, these taxes apply to goods that are useful in production rather than to "bads" such as pollution. They may well distort incentives away from efficient methods of production rather than improve incentives by discouraging pollution.

Second, these taxes raise the cost of production and thus raise equilibrium output prices. An incentive-based tax on smokestack emissions would raise the cost of producing certain goods, but then those goods are used as inputs to the production of other goods. The ultimate burden becomes diffuse. Similarly, actual U.S. taxes apply to goods like chemicals, petroleum, and coal that are inputs to virtually all other industries. The calculations presented in this paper use an input–output model to find the effect of actual environmental taxes on 41 output prices. Taxes apply to 9 of the intermediate inputs, at rates up to 7 percent, but they raise the cost of production for all 41 outputs. Most prices rise by less than 1 percent, and the largest increase is 2 percent. Thus, the ultimate burdens are similar to those of a broad-based tax. Separate environmental taxes are not effective at targeting burdens on those responsible for pollution, except to the extent that all of us are responsible. The objective of fairness may be equally met by broad-based taxes.

Third, the evidence on administrative and compliance costs strongly suggests economies of scale in the collection of revenue. Each tax requires its own set of forms, its own administrative structure, and its own calculation of the tax base for each taxpayer. Those calculations are the same whether the tax base is multiplied by a low tax rate or a high tax rate. Thus, the compliance cost as a fraction of revenue will tend to be high at tax rates that are low. Yet each separate environmental tax in the United States collects revenue for a separate cleanup program that represents a very small fraction of the total federal budget. Each rate of tax is typically less than 1 percent. Thus, these taxes have a relatively high compliance cost per dollar of revenue.

When the three pieces of this puzzle come together, an interesting pattern emerges. A separate environmental tax might be effective at discouraging a particular polluting activity, even if it requires its own administrative structure and has a relatively high compliance cost per dollar of revenue. But actual environmental taxes do not follow that logic. Separate environmental taxes are used not for incentives but to target burdens on particular industries thought to be responsible. Each tax funds the cleanup of a particular pollution problem, applies at a low rate, and has a relatively high compliance cost. But burdens cannot be targeted. The same revenue could be collected, with the same diffuse burdens, using an existing broad-based tax instrument with a much lower compliance cost per dollar of revenue. The analysis points toward better use of incentive-based environmental taxes or the funding of cleanup programs using general revenues.

2. THE DESIGN OF ENVIRONMENTAL TAXES

Policymakers are torn by trade-offs among competing policy objectives. This section briefly describes at least a dozen such objectives, whereas the rest of the paper concentrates on the first three. First, a tax can be used to increase economic efficiency by discouraging an activity that causes environmental harm. In theory, the total welfare of society is maximized by continuing a production activity until social marginal benefit falls to the level of social marginal cost. If some pollutant generates external costs not recognized by the firm, then the activity may continue beyond that point, until marginal benefit falls to the level of purely private marginal cost. This behavior can be restrained either by traditional command and control regulations that tell the firm to cut back, or by incentive-based policies that induce the firm to cut back. As suggested by Pigou (1932), a tax on emissions can make the firm recognize the full social cost of its actions. Ideally, the Pigouvian tax would apply not to the output of the industry but to the part of the production process that causes the pollution. For example, a tax on hazardous waste would provide incentives to change not just the input of chemicals, but the nature of their use and the generation of hazardous waste by-products. Such taxes raise the cost of production, and higher prices might discourage purchase of the output, but they also provide incentives for the firm to reduce the pollution per unit of output. Such taxes might improve on command and control regulations by inducing firms to find the minimum cost method of controlling waste emissions: each firm can decide whether it is cheaper to scrap the old process for a new technology, switch inputs, buy control equipment, or pay the tax.

Thus, the "polluter pays" can be interpreted as a principle of economic efficiency, where the objective of the tax is to collect a marginal price per unit of pollution. But it can also be interpreted as a principle of fairness, where the objective of the tax is to collect appropriate total amounts from the parties responsible for the pollution. A tax might be used to achieve this second objective without the first. An example is the U.S. tax on chemical feedstocks (intermediate inputs). This tax is devoted to the cleanup of abandoned contaminated sites under the Superfund program, and it may well collect from the firms responsible for that pollution. But this tax on the input of chemicals does not provide incentives to change the use of those chemicals, reduce the generation of waste, or dispose of that waste safely. It does not discourage the abandonment of contaminated sites.

The goal of fairness might also involve distributional effects more generally, including the ultimate burdens of the tax on different income groups.

A third goal is to minimize administrative costs to government and compliance costs to taxpayers. Increased complexity usually requires more instructions, more time filling out forms, and more difficult audits. Yet some complexity might be necessary to identify particular polluting activities. A tax on hazardous waste would better discourage polluting behavior, but taxes on chemical feedstocks and petroleum are probably easier to administer and still collect from the waste-generating firms. Another complication is that the administrative cost of using taxes to protect the environment really should be compared with the analogous administrative costs of using alternative command and control policies to regulate polluting behavior.

Some other objectives should at least be mentioned.[1] A fourth goal is

---

[1] A large literature discusses the choice among policy options: see Bohm and Russell (1985), Baumol and Oates (1988), Merrill and Rousso (1991), or Barthold (1994).

to avoid problems of information and measurement. The ideal incentive-based tax rate would reflect the marginal external cost of pollution, but this cost is difficult to measure, since it may require the probable number and cost of illnesses, the dollar value of lives lost, and the aggregate willingness to pay for greater visibility. Yet actual environmental tax rates are not set on this basis at all. Each tax is set instead at a rate that will yield a prespecified revenue for a trust fund. For example, Superfund taxes pay for the costs of cleaning up existing contaminated sites, costs that bear no relation to the external cost of using more new chemicals or petroleum.

A fifth goal is the flexibility to adjust tax rules as information and measurement improve or as the situation changes. On the other hand, a sixth goal is to provide business with a more certain set of tax rates so as not to change the rules in the middle of the game. Seventh, the policy needs to reflect monitoring capabilities. A Pigouvian tax may require counting tons of emissions, whereas a design standard simply requires authorities to confirm the use of a particular kind of pollution control equipment. An eighth goal is political feasibility. A regulation can "guarantee" certain pollution controls, whereas a tax must rely on the theory that firms will be induced to cut pollution. Also, existing firms may provide more support for a plan to allocate tradable permits than for a plan to tax all emissions. A ninth, related objective involves ethics. One view is that pollution is a "crime against nature" that ought to be stigmatized by legal regulations rather than condoned by the mere payment of a tax. Tenth, policymakers must worry about the costs of a transition to a new system of taxation, including unemployment, moving costs, and retraining. Yet another objective is to account for methods of avoidance or evasion. A tax applied to each unit of waste brought to a qualified disposal facility might be designed to reflect the social harm from that waste and to discourage generation of waste, but it might just shift disposal away from the qualified facilities and toward improper methods of disposal that can cause worse environmental harm.[2] Finally, the implementation of a Pigouvian tax might be complicated by the concern for other policy goals related to issues, such as market structure, monopoly power, trade agreements, and international competitiveness.

No tax can meet all twelve of these objectives. It might be possible to identify certain reforms, however, that can achieve more of one objective without significant losses elsewhere. In particular, since existing U.S.

---

[2] In some cases, evasion is easy. A tanker truck filled with waste can enter a truck wash, get all the washer sprays going, and then open the drain on the bottom of the truck. Another example is that waste oil can easily go undetected if dumped on roadbeds of railroad lines.

environmental taxes are not designed for incentives anyway, an alternative broad-based tax may have the same diffuse burdens with less compliance cost.

3. ADMINISTRATIVE AND COMPLIANCE COST

The Internal Revenue Service (IRS) budget is about $6 billion per year, which includes spending on equipment and rent as well as salaries of clerks, auditors, and lawyers. This administrative cost is less than 0.6 percent of total federal receipts ($1.09 trillion in 1992). Thus, the U.S. is fairly efficient at collecting taxes. The IRS cannot break down their costs of collecting each tax.

The reason that the U.S. government has relatively low collection costs is that it puts most of the cost on the taxpayers. The compliance cost to taxpayers includes not only the dollars paid to accountants and lawyers, but the value of all time spent keeping receipts, reading instructions, and filling out forms. For the individual income tax, Slemrod and Sorum (1984) estimate for 1982 that "between 1.8 and 2.1 billion hours of taxpayer time were spent on filing tax returns, and between $3.0 and $3.4 billion was spent on professional tax assistance." Taxpayer time is valued at the net wage rate for a total compliance cost of 5 to 7 percent of revenue. Thus, the compliance cost of the income tax is ten times the administrative cost to the IRS.

3.1 Economies of Scale

Both logic and evidence suggest that many of these administrative and compliance costs are "fixed" costs of calculating the tax base, not marginal costs of collecting more revenue by raising the rate of tax on a given tax base. Compliance costs depend on the complexity and number of forms to be filed by taxpayers, just as administrative costs depend on the number of forms to be checked by the IRS. Under the income tax, different forms are required for itemized deductions, depreciation calculations, and each type of income, such as interest, dividends, capital gains, rental income, and self-employment income. The last step is to multiply this tax base times a tax rate, or just look up the tax in a table provided by the IRS, a step that is equally simple whether that tax rate is 1 or 30 percent. Thus, the technology of tax collections exhibits economies of scale. The administrative cost or compliance cost as a fraction of tax revenue is expected to fall as the tax rate and revenue becomes larger.

The same economies hold for excise taxes. When the United Kingdom increased the value-added tax (VAT) rate from 8 to 15 percent in 1979, for example, Sandford, Godwin, and Hardwick (1989) found that "over the next few years the [administrative] cost : revenue ratio in the collection of the VAT fell from 2 percent to one percent mainly, though not solely, because of the increase in rate" (p. 20).

Sandford, Godwin, and Hardwick (1989) find further evidence of economies of scale by looking at firms of different sizes. For 1986–1987 in the United Kingdom, the cost of complying with the VAT as a percent of the tax base was smaller for businesses that were larger, as measured either by the tax base or by the number of employees (p. 142). Similar results were found for the goods and services tax (GST) in Canada by Plamondon and Associates, Inc. (1993) and for the corporation income tax in the United States by Slemrod and Blumenthal (1993).[3] Although this type of scale economy pertains to firm size rather than tax rate, the implication still is that compliance cost includes a fixed annual amount that depends on the number and complexity of forms used to calculate the tax base.

If the only goal were to raise a small additional amount of revenue for a trust fund, this analysis suggests a small increase in a preexisting excise tax rate, corporate income tax rate, or even personal income tax rates. If a special tax must be introduced, the revenue would be collected most efficiently with a single tax rate on a relatively simple tax base.

3.2 An Estimate of Compliance Cost for the Corporate Environmental Tax

The Superfund's corporate environmental tax (CET) is not an excise tax at all. It applies at a 0.12 percent rate on a measure of income that is related to the alternative minimum tax (AMT), regardless of whether that firm is actually subject to the AMT.[4] Revenue is about a half a billion dollars, but compliance is complicated.

To calculate the AMT, the firm starts with its regular taxable income and adds back net operating loss deductions, "adjustments," and "preference" items, such as interest from certain tax-exempt bonds. The "adjustments" include the difference between depreciation according to regular tax schedules and depreciation according to AMT rules. Thus,

---

[3] Slemrod and Blumenthal (1993) say that their "tables 10 through 15 suggest that, in general, compliance costs rise less than proportionately with firm size, so that average costs per unit of size, however measured, are lower for larger firms. . . . The findings of economies of scale in tax compliance costs is common in studies across countries and across types of tax" (p. 6).

[4] The AMT was created in 1986 to ensure that taxpayers with substantial incomes could not avoid paying taxes through "excessive" use of deductions, tax credits, and other exclusions permitted under the law.

for each asset it purchases, the firm must keep track of one depreciation schedule for book purposes, another for the regular tax, and a third for the AMT. Also, deductions are cut back for mining costs, intangible drilling costs, and pollution control facilities (see Lyon, 1991, pp. 51–82). Then the AMT requires an additional calculation of profits, termed adjusted current earnings (ACE).

The firm calculates regular tax as 35 percent of corporate taxable income, and then it calculates the tentative minimum tax as 20 percent of AMT income (AMTI), a broader definition of income. It pays AMT equal to the excess of tentative minimum tax over regular tax, if any.

Regardless of whether the firm pays the AMT, the CET applies at a 0.12 percent rate to the "modified" AMTI in excess of $2 million, where the AMTI is modified to disallow deductions for net operating losses and for the CET itself.

If all firms had to calculate the AMTI anyway, then the CET would not introduce much additional compliance cost. Of the 12,199 firms that paid the CET in 1990, however, 8,584 (70 percent) did not pay the AMT.[5] The additional costs to these firms of complying with the CET can be substantial, if they are anything like the cost of complying with the AMT estimated by Slemrod and Blumenthal (1993). They surveyed 365 large corporations and found that their average cost of corporate income tax compliance was $1.57 million (p. 5). Using the 365 observations, they regressed compliance cost on certain firm characteristics and found that

Being subject to the alternative minimum tax (AMT) adds 16.9 percent; this is true even though all but three of the firms report that they must calculate the alternative minimum tax liability. This result implies that those firms that suspect that they will actually have AMT liability devote more resources to its calculation and planning implications [pp. 7–8].

In other words, almost all firms make initial calculations to determine whether they are subject to the AMT, but the extra 16.9 percent of compliance cost is incurred only by firms that really are subject to AMT. Presumably they review calculations carefully and undertake more tax planning.[6] This additional compliance cost is 16.9 percent of $1.57 million, or $265,330 per firm. This figure is used by Probst et al. (1995) to provide a rough estimate of CET compliance costs.

---

[5] Phone conversation with Patty Treubert, IRS, Statistics of Income Division, May 1994.

[6] The regression results may also reflect greater complexity of firms that pay the AMT.

First, however, consider the Slemrod and Blumenthal (1993) estimates. The $1.57 million of compliance cost seems large, but they look only at very large firms. In fact, 98 of their 365 firms are in the Fortune 500 largest industrial firms in the United States. For these large firms, the estimated compliance cost is a reasonable 3 percent of total taxes paid. Second, Slemrod and Blumenthal (1993) find that AMT calculations cost 17 percent more. This figure seems low, if anything, since the AMT is a parallel tax system that essentially doubles the number of calculations necessary to obtain taxable income, allowable deductions, and tax due. Thus, the $265,330 is a very believable cost of AMT compliance for these firms.

Third, consider what the cost of AMT compliance indicates about the cost of CET compliance. All large firms perform rough calculations to determine AMT liability, so the $265,330 represents the incremental cost of actually having to pay the AMT. The same increment would represent the cost of having to pay the CET if the calculations are performed properly, since the same tax base is used for both. On the other hand, compliance costs include tax planning costs, which may increase with the tax rate. In other words, firms may expend more effort to reduce the AMT at the 20 percent rate than to reduce the CET at the 0.12 percent rate.

Fourth, consider whether the firms studied by Slemrod and Blumenthal (1993) are representative of firms that pay the CET. The firms surveyed are large, but so are the firms that pay the CET, since the CET applies only to the extent that the AMTI exceeds 2 million dollars. Of 3.7 million corporate tax returns in 1990, the IRS reports that only 5,589 (0.15 percent) are what they call giants, firms with more than $250 million of assets. Of 32,462 firms that pay the AMT, however, 1,324 (4 percent) are "giants." Even more striking is that 3,131 of the 12,199 firms that pay the CET—a full 25 percent—are giants.[7]

Finally, consider which of these firms could be said to incur the extra $265,330 compliance cost. Of the 8,584 firms that pay the CET but not the AMT, the IRS reports that 1,952 (23 percent) are giants. If the $265,330 cost applies only to these 1,952 "giants" that pay the CET and not the AMT, the compliance cost would be $518 million. This compliance cost is 100 percent of total CET revenue.[8] This estimate is meant to be conserva-

---

[7] These figures were all reported in a phone conversation by Patty Treubert, IRS, Statistics of Income Division, May 1994.

[8] Others have suggested that "the cost of computing the CET could be greater than the current tax liability" for some companies (see Price Waterhouse, 1992, p. 47.).

tive, since it totally ignores the compliance cost for the (12,199 − 1,952 =) 10,247 firms that are not giants or that already pay the AMT.[9]

Even this estimate may seem implausibly large, but note that the $265,330 compliance cost represents only the annual cost of one accountant and one tax lawyer, a moderate allocation of personnel for one of these giant corporations. This cost is attributed only to the largest 1,952 of the 12,199 firms that pay the CETs. Instead, the same total estimated compliance cost ($518 million) can be expressed as an average of $42,462 for all of the 12,199 firms that pay the CET. The problem is not that this compliance cost is so large, but that the revenue is so small, also only $42,462 per firm.[10]

The CET was not designed to discourage polluting activities nor to target its burden on those responsible. Rather, it was intended to raise some money for the cleanup of contaminated sites under the Superfund. But an additional collection mechanism is not necessary to raise some money for cleanup.

4. SOME ACTUAL ENVIRONMENTAL TAXES

The IRS *Statistics of Income* identifies four "environmental" taxes on (1) petroleum, for the Oil Spill Liability Trust Fund (OSLTF) and the Superfund; (2) chemical feedstocks, for the Superfund; (3) ozone-depleting chemicals, for the general fund; and (4) motor fuels, for the Leaky Underground Storage Tank (LUST) fund.[11] Table 1 summarizes the rates and revenues from some components of these explicitly environmental taxes. Each is discussed further later. Table 1 also summarizes some other federal excise taxes that are likely to have environmental effects, such as taxes on coal, tires, gasoline, trucks and trailers, gas guzzlers, and transportation. These taxes probably discourage the use of fossil fuels that cause air pollution and global warming, but they are not labeled as environmental taxes because they do not feed a trust fund used to clean up the environment.

---

[9] The firms studied by Slemrod and Blumenthal (1993) may be even larger, on average, than these 1,952 giants. Microdata are not available to make use of the estimated coefficient on size. The $265,330 estimate may be a bit high even for these 1,952 firms, but this bias is probably more than offset by ignoring the compliance cost of the other 10,247 firms that pay the CET.

[10] The CET is complex, but at least it uses the existing definition of the AMTI. Some proposed alternatives would have invented a whole new tax base.

[11] The IRS lists many excise taxes that might affect the environment, like the gasoline tax for the Highway Trust Fund, but the category for "environmental" excise taxes includes only the four listed here, as discussed by Davie (1995) and Poterba and Rotemberg (1995).

TABLE 1
Federal Environmental Tax Rates, Revenues, and Numbers of Taxpayers

Tax	Statutory rate, 1992	Revenue, $ millions, 1992	Number of taxpayers	Revenue ($000) per taxpayer
Explicit environmental taxes				
Petroleum, for Oil Spill Liability	$0.05/barrel	273.8	312[a]	877.6
Petroleum, for Superfund	$0.097/barrel	552.9	341[a]	1,621.4
Chemicals, for Superfund	$0.22–4.87/ton	252.2	452	558.0
Imported chemical substances, for Superfund	Various/ton	16.5	138	119.6
Ozone-depleting chemicals, for GF	$0.0205–1.67/pound	558.2	695	803.2
Floor stocks of ozone-depleting chemicals, for GF	$0.18–0.30/pound	9.9	1,440	6.9
Some implicit environmental taxes				
Coal, mined underground, for Black Lung Disability	$1.10/ton or 4.4% of value	410.6	779	527.1
Coal, surface mined, for Black Lung Disability	$0.55/ton or 4.4% of value	220.0	975	225.6

Tires, for HTF	$0.15–0.50/pound	279.9	216	1,295.8
Pistols and revolvers, for Wildlife Restoration Account	10% of value	43.4	754	57.6
Gasoline, for HTF[b]	$0.141/gallon	14,759.3	5696	2,591.2
Diesel fuel, for HTF[b]	$0.201/gallon	4,071.9	22,611	180.1
Heavy trucks and trailers, for HTF	12% of value	904.9	3,226	280.5
Gas guzzlers, for HTF	Up to $7,700/vehicle	144.2	98	1,471.4
Transportation by air, for Airport and Airway Trust Fund[c]	10% of value	4,173.5	1,505	2,773.1
Use tax on heavy vehicles, for HTF	Up to $550/vehicle/year	596.2	3,226	184.8

Source: Davie (1993) and the author's calculations.

[a] This number is the sum of the numbers of taxpayers who pay domestic petroleum tax and imported petroleum tax. Some firms may be counted twice, but they do have to pay two separate taxes and file separate forms.

[b] The model used in section 6 (and described in the appendix) includes other smaller taxes on gasohol, commercial and noncommercial aviation fuels, and special motor fuels. All these revenues are split among the Highway Trust Fund (HTF), Airport and Airway Trust Fund, Aquatic Resources Trust Fund, Leaking Underground Storage Tank (LUST) Trust Fund, and the General Fund (GF).

[c] The model includes other smaller taxes on transportation of property by air (also for Airport and Airway Trust Fund), transportation by water (GF), railroads, and aviation (LUST).

This is only a partial list. Barthold (1994) provides a useful table of 51 federal tax code provisions that might affect the environment, including other excise taxes as well as federal income tax provisions, such as credits for nonconventional fuels, reforestation, and closed-loop biomass production. The income tax also affects the environment through its treatment of commuting expenses, depletion allowances, intangible drilling expenses, mine exploration expenses, pollution control equipment, and capital gains from timber sales.[12] Analysis here is limited to the excise taxes listed in Table 1.

4.1 Petroleum Tax

An oil refiner is required to pay tax when domestic crude petroleum is received at a U.S. refinery, and an importer must pay tax when crude oil and refined petroleum products enter the United States. Table 1 shows that in 1992 the OSLTF received 5 cents per barrel, and the Hazardous Substance Superfund received 9.7 cents per barrel, so the combined tax on crude petroleum was 14.7 cents per barrel. At a price of about $20 per barrel, crude oil was effectively taxed at a rate of about 0.7 or 0.8 percent. The combined tax collected $827 million in 1992, which is only 0.076 percent of federal receipts ($1.09 trillion in 1992).[13]

This tax is small, but its operation is simple. Table 1 shows that it applies to only 341 firms. The last column divides tax revenue by the number of taxpaying firms, as a very rough indicator of compliance cost efficiency. For the Superfund tax on petroleum, the compliance cost per firm must be much less than the average revenue of $1.6 million per firm.

The revenue is used to clean up toxic waste, and Congress attempted to target the burden on those responsible. For the initial legislation in 1980, a survey of the chemical composition of hazardous waste sites was used to determine that 15 percent was derived from petroleum, 65 percent from petrochemicals, and 20 percent from inorganic substances. The total revenue requirement was divided in these proportions, and

---

[12] Barthold (1994) also describes several reasons for separate environmental taxes. First, a Pigouvian tax would discourage pollution. Second, the benefit principle suggests a "user fee," or tax that reflects benefits from using a public environmental resource. Third, a tax can represent a mandated "insurance premium" for risk pooling, such as the tax on petroleum that is used to clean up oil spills. A problem is that oil companies cannot draw on this fund in case of accident; it is only for costs that cannot be recovered from liable firms.

[13] The oil spill portion of the tax was suspended on July 1, 1993 (because the trust fund achieved its target of $1 billion), and it expired on December 31, 1994. The remaining 9.7 cent Superfund tax represents less than one half of 1 percent of the petroleum price.

then the projected size of each tax base was used to determine the tax rate that would collect the desired revenue from each source.[14]

This rationale has a number of problems. First, even if this tax applies to the responsible firms, it cannot apply to the managers or shareholders responsible for this past pollution because those individuals have long since changed jobs or sold their stock in the company. The burden of the tax could at best apply to new managers and shareholders who had nothing to do with the existing abandoned contaminated sites. Second, even if the legislated burdens on these firms are passed on to customers through higher prices, the customers may not be the same individuals who benefited from artificially low prices in the past. Third, the tax does nothing to discourage the abandonment of contaminated sites. It applies to petroleum as an input to production, not to any waste by-product that gives rise to external cost. Other environmental regulations are designed to control the handling of waste from production processes that use petroleum. Similarly, as noted by Barthold (1994), the OSLTF tax on petroleum did not apply to oil spills or to behavior that might cause spills. It applied at the same rate to all oil, whether transported by pipeline, in single-hulled tankers, or in double-hulled tankers that are more difficult to rupture.

The petroleum tax might have some incentive effects that are favorable to the environment if it discourages the use of petroleum that is correlated to the burning of petroleum-based fuels or the runoff from petroleum-based fertilizers. But these goals could be better achieved by taxes on the appropriate fuels and fertilizers, if not directly on the emissions and runoff.

4.2 Chemical Feedstock Taxes

Another federal excise tax is imposed on the sale or use of 42 organic and inorganic chemical feedstocks (intermediate inputs), whether domestic or imported. The revenue is devoted to the Superfund. The tax rates were originally set in 1980 at $4.87 per ton for organic chemicals and at similar rates per ton for inorganic chemicals.[15] Since then, individual rates have been modified. Whereas the petroleum tax collected $553 million with a single rate on one commodity, Table 1 shows that the chemical feedstock taxes collected $252 million using 42 rates on 42

---

[14] See the July 11, 1980, report of the Senate Committee on Environment and Public Works, regarding S. 1480, as described in Price Waterhouse (1992) Appendix A, note 23.

[15] Inorganic chemicals are taxed at $0.17 per ton plus $4.28 per ton times the portion of molecular weight deemed to be attributable to hazardous elements. The total tax rate was limited to 2 percent of the wholesale price in 1980 (see Price Waterhouse, 1992, Appendix A).

different commodities.[16] The complications are illustrated by the fact that a different set of chemicals is exempt under each of the following circumstances: if used in the manufacture of certain motor fuels; if used in making certain fertilizer; if produced as a by-product of air pollution control devices; if existing only temporarily in the smelting or refining of nontaxed chemicals; if coal-derived feedstocks; if a separated isomer of xylene; if recovered from certain recycling processes; if used to produce a qualified animal feed substance; if part of an intermediate hydrocarbon stream; or if exported (Commerce Clearing House, 1995, pp. 210–213).

In 1986, to avoid putting domestic producers at a competitive disadvantage, Congress added taxes on the import of 50 chemical substances produced using chemical feedstocks that are taxed in the United States. The rate on each of these substances is meant to reflect the tax that would have been paid on the chemical feedstocks used in its production. This law also directs the Secretary of the Treasury to augment this list with additional substances demonstrated to contain taxed chemicals that constitute 50 percent of the product by weight or by value. Since that time, at least 77 additional imported chemical substances have been added to the list. Despite imposing 127 different tax rates on 127 different imported chemical substances, these taxes together collected only $16.5 million in 1992, as shown in Table 1. This amount is about 1 percent of the total Superfund tax, which itself is about 0.1 percent of total federal revenue.

If this tax had any benefit in terms of revenue or competitiveness, that benefit is swamped by administrative complexity. Because the chemical feedstock tax does not apply to exports, the IRS must establish procedures to refund the right amount of tax on an export produced using the taxed input. Then the IRS must continually consider petitions to add to the list, from exporters who want refunds and from others who want taxes on imported goods with which they compete.

The original motivation for these taxes was related to Superfund sites contaminated not by these chemicals themselves, but by toxic waste byproducts that were generated by the use of these chemicals in complex

---

[16] Several of the 42 rates are the same. All excise taxes appear on IRS Form 720, with one set of instructions and one line for "chemicals," but the individual chemicals are listed on Form 6627 for "environmental taxes." A firm that must pay tax on two of these commodities clearly incurs less than twice the compliance cost of a firm that must pay tax on one. The main problem with taxing any additional commodity is that it may increase the number of firms that must file the forms. The IRS estimates the average firm's time requirements for recordkeeping at twenty-five hours, twenty-one minutes, learning about the forms at two hours, twenty-six minutes, and preparing forms at eight hours, fifty-two minutes.

compound forms (Fullerton and Tsang, 1993). Toxicity depends on what the firms do with the chemicals.

4.3 Ozone-Depleting Chemicals

The Montreal Protocol is an international agreement to phase out the use of halons and chlorofluorocarbons (CFCs) that deplete the layer of stratospheric ozone protecting the Earth from the harmful ultraviolet rays of the sun. Halons are used in fire extinguishers and CFCs in air conditioners. The agreement sets phased quantity restrictions and lets individual nations decide how to meet them. The U.S. uses a combination of quantity regulations and taxes. The tax rate on each chemical is determined by a base tax amount (which started at $1.37 per pound in 1989) times an "ozone-depleting factor" (which was set at 1.0 for CFC-12 and which varies from 0.1 for methyl chloroform to 10.0 for halon-1301). The number of taxed chemicals has grown to 20, and the initial base tax amount has grown to $5.35 per pound in 1995. It will increase by another $0.45 per pound every year.

This tax is not retrospective like other environmental taxes that finance a cleanup fund by collecting from those responsible for some past pollution problem. This tax does not feed a trust fund. It is prospective, since it helps prevent further harm by reducing the future use of ozone-depleting chemicals. It applies fairly closely to the activity causing environmental harm, and it even applies at a rate that varies with the degree of environmental harm.

Yet Congress did not intend to use incentives for the environment. Instead, quantity restrictions on manufacturers were designed to meet the quantity targets in the Montreal Protocol. Congress then noticed that quantity restrictions can lead to monopoly profits. The tax rate was set equal to the expected difference between the new equilibrium price and the cost of production (Merrill and Rousso, 1991). In other words, this tax was enacted as a windfall profits tax rather than as a Pigouvian tax. Congress was concerned with fairness and revenue, not incentives.

Producers reacted by cutting production below the levels mandated by the Montreal Protocol.[17] Since the quantity restriction is not binding, the tax unintentionally became the operational tool for reducing use of ozone-depleting chemicals.[18]

---

[17] Barthold (1994) considers the case of ozone-depleting chemicals in great detail. He points out that the quantity control could be viewed as a "backstop that is reassuring to those who doubt the efficacy of the price system" (p. 135).

[18] Other aspects of the tax are not ideal for incentives. As just described, the tax rate was not set by looking at the environmental damage per unit of chemical. Also, the tax applies to production and use of these chemicals, whereas environmental damage occurs only on

Any time that a tax is imposed on a particular commodity, or in this case twenty, Congress has to worry about several issues that complicate the operation of the tax. First, rules and exemptions must be specified for each chemical. Second, the tax is imposed on manufacturers rather than the more numerous purchasers of these chemicals; but then the imposition of the tax can be avoided by selling off inventories in anticipation of the effective date. To prevent this transitional problem, Congress often imposes a special tax on floor stocks held by purchasers on the date that such a tax is enacted or increased. Table 1 shows that the tax on floor stocks of ozone-depleting chemicals raised only $9.9 million in 1992 but applied to 1,440 firms, so the average is only $6,900 per taxpayer.[19] The tax on floor stocks is shown for ozone-depleting chemicals only in Table 1, but similar rules have applied to the imposition of taxes on virtually any type of commodity.

Third, Congress is concerned with international competitiveness and feels compelled to tax each import at a rate that reflects the tax that would have been paid on the input to its production if it had been produced in the United States (Davie, 1995). The Superfund tax on imported chemical substances was described earlier, but a similar logic applies to ozone-depleting chemicals. Poterba and Rotemberg (1995) analyze the logic of this extra corrective tax and show that it is impossible to implement it in the common case where final goods are produced as joint products. The point here is that even if imperfect rules are implemented, using arbitrary assumptions about foreign production, they are bound to be complicated.

Finally, some of these complications can be avoided by ignoring small amounts, but Congress prohibited the Treasury from creating *de minimus* exemptions for electronics (Barthold, 1994). Thus, the tax on import of goods produced using ozone-depleting chemicals is most often below 1 percent and is only 0.03 percent for fax machines, camcorders, and radios (Davie, 1995).

4.4 Motor Fuels

The fourth and final explicit environmental tax is a tiny $0.001 per gallon tax on gasoline and other motor fuels that finances the trust fund used to

---

their release into the atmosphere (Barthold, 1994). Halons are never released from fire extinguishers that are never used, and CFCs are not released from air conditioners if the CFCs are properly recaptured for later use. For this reason, Bohm (1981) has suggested the use of a deposit–refund system that would rebate the tax on CFCs that are captured and returned.

[19] Although their own revenue is small, floor stock taxes may prevent the loss of excise tax revenues from manufacturers selling more inventories before the effective date.

clean up leaky underground storage tanks for which no solvent owner can be found. Fortunately, this small tax is attached to other more substantial taxes on gasoline and other motor fuels. The overall tax rate on gasoline is now $.184 per gallon, and the rate on diesel fuel is $.244 per gallon. Substitute fuels such as gasohol are taxed at lower rates to encourage conservation of fossil fuels.

The gasoline tax is about the best available example of an incentive-based environmental tax (even though it is not called an environmental tax because it does not finance a cleanup program). Gasoline is a well-defined commodity to tax, and the revenue is substantial. This tax collected almost $15 billion in 1992, as shown in Table 1. It has incentive effects favorable to the environment, since it might help to conserve energy and improve air quality.

It is still a highly imperfect example, however. Its original intent was not as an incentive-based tax, but as a user fee to collect from those who benefit from public spending on highways. Most of it still finances the Highway Trust Fund, used for highway construction. Its incentives are weaker than one might think. Environmental damages result from emissions, and gasoline is only weakly correlated to emissions. Walls and Hanson (1995) describe how emission rates vary greatly across vehicle age, vehicle maintenance, and styles of driving. In a study of a scrappage program, Alberini et al. (1994) find that pre-1980 vehicles currently have an average tailpipe hydrocarbon emission rate (6.6 grams per mile) that is 26 times the current new car standard (0.25 grams per mile). Even a relatively new car might have many times its original emission rate if its pollution control equipment is broken. Because of emissions from cold start-ups, Burmich (1989) finds that a 5-mile trip has almost three times the emissions per mile as a 20-mile trip at the same speed. Sierra Research (1994) finds that a car driven aggressively has a carbon monoxide emission rate (39 grams per mile) that is almost 20 times higher than when driven normally (2.2 grams per mile). The gasoline tax does not have incentives to scrap high-emission cars, fix broken emission equipment, or drive less aggressively.

Finally, some peculiar exemptions add considerable unnecessary complexity. Since it is a fee on users of highways, the special motor fuels tax (even the LUST portion) does not apply to "off-highway business use," such as fisheries and whaling businesses, but "off-highway use" does not include motorboats or diesel-powered trains; use in farming; sales to museums that operate exclusively for the care of World War II aircraft; sales to state and local governments and to Indian tribal governments; certain diplomatic uses; sales to nonprofit educational institutions; and use of a helicopter for the exploration or development of minerals, oil, or gas, or in logging operations or emergency medical services, unless the helicopter takes off or lands at an airport eligible for federal assistance (Commerce Clearing House, 1995, pp. 50–53). These exemptions are designed to target burdens, not environmental incentives.

4.5 Other Implicit Environmental Taxes

Besides those four explicit environmental taxes, Table 1 lists a number of other taxes likely to have environmental effects. These taxes might feed a trust fund (but not for a cleanup program like the explicit environmental taxes). The tax rates on coal in 1995 are the same as those in 1992, as shown in Table 1, when the combined revenue was $630 million (0.06 percent of total federal receipts). This tax might discourage some use of fossil fuels, but it was designed to place a burden on those who benefit from the use of the Black Lung Disability Trust Fund.

The small ($43 million per year) tax on pistols and revolvers might be called environmental, since it feeds the Wildlife Restoration Account, but it was designed as a user fee on those who benefit from that account. To the extent that it discourages the use of guns, it might be said to correct a negative externality. The tax code includes a plethora of other excise taxes that might discourage driving and other use of fossil fuels, such as taxes on tires, on heavy trucks and trailers, on air transportation of persons and property, and on vehicles shown to have low mileage per gallon ("gas guzzlers"). A few of these taxes are listed in Table 1. Section 6 considers whether the many separate taxes have any separate effects on tax burdens.

5. A CASE STUDY OF AN INCENTIVE-BASED TAX THAT FAILED

The incentive-based tax inevitably conflicts with other goals of policymakers. Consider a waste-end tax. First, the waste reduction itself conflicts with the tax revenue goal, since it erodes the tax base and reduces revenue. For this reason, waste reduction has most often been omitted from any list of goals for actual waste-end taxes in the past.

Second, the waste-end tax may conflict with the goal of fairness if it is used to clean up an existing contaminated site, since it collects from generators of new waste and from those who use proper (taxable) disposal methods, not from those who generated the past waste that was improperly handled at the existing contaminated site.

Third, a waste-end tax may conflict with the goal of minimizing administrative costs. It may be particularly difficult to implement for lack of data on the number of hazardous waste generators or the amount of each type of waste generated.[20] It may be difficult to administer and to enforce because of easy opportunities for avoidance. Firms may use cheap on-site disposal methods that are hard to capture within the purview of the tax, and they might use other, outright illegal methods, such as midnight dumping. The usual tax administration and compliance cost is augmented by significant noncompliance costs.[21]

Consider the reasoning behind the federal waste-end tax originally enacted in 1980 and behind its repeal in 1986.[22] The 1980 legislation not only established the Hazardous Substance Response Trust Fund (later known as the Superfund) to deal with contaminated sites, but it also established the Post-Closure Liability Trust Fund (PCLTF) to ensure continued long-term monitoring and care at other closed hazardous waste disposal facilities. To qualify for this program, a facility must receive a permit under the Resource Conservation and Recovery Act (RCRA), operate in compliance with the RCRA, continue monitoring for 5 years after closing, and demonstrate no substantial likelihood of any future release of hazardous substances. After the 5-year period, the federal government would assume any future liability (including third-party claims, not covered under the Superfund). The PCLTF was financed by a tax on hazardous waste that would remain at qualified facilities, at a rate of $2.13 per dry-weight ton. This tax would not be imposed during any year in which the balance in the fund exceeded $200 million.

The PCLTF was intended to encourage firms to comply with the RCRA and not to abandon sites on closure. The fund would help to avoid future health hazards, increase the chances of detecting releases promptly, and ensure that funds would be available to pay remaining

---

[20] See Carlson and Bausell (1987). They also evaluate several waste-end tax options. McNeil and Foshee (1988) compare a tax on waste disposal to a tax on waste generation.

[21] These noncompliance costs can be reduced by replacing the waste-end tax with a "deposit-refund" system. Bohm (1981) and Fullerton and Kinnaman (1995) describe such a system. First, it would collect tax on each firm's purchase of any substance that is potentially polluting, at a rate that reflects the external cost of illegal disposal of that substance. Second, it would then rebate those taxes according to the amounts of those substances that exit the firm through sales of final products, leaving no tax on substances that do not appear as waste. Third, it would rebate part of the original tax on any item that exits the firm by qualified disposal methods. The part of the tax that is not rebated could reflect the social external cost of disposal that takes place even by qualified methods at qualified sites. The entire tax would remain on substances appearing neither in sales nor in qualified disposal methods—presumably illegal disposal. Such systems may be difficult to implement, but they are not as difficult as taxing illegal disposal directly.

[22] The Comprehensive Environmental Response, Compensation, and Liability Act (CERCLA) was enacted in 1980 and the Superfund Amendments and Reauthorization Act (SARA) in 1986.

claims (U.S. Environmental Protection Agency [EPA], 1985, p. 13). The tax, of course, was intended to finance the fund. It follows the "polluter pays" principle by collecting from firms that generate the wastes that entail the risk of future health or property damage. Note, however, that this list of goals omits any mention of using the tax to reduce the generation of such waste.

This fund and waste-end tax had a long list of problems that let to its repeal. First, the legislation never defined a "dry-weight ton." Presumably, the intent was to exclude the water component of different wastes in order to make them comparable, but it certainly left an administrative complexity. Second, the tax base excluded a lot of waste that is never sent to a qualified facility but is instead managed on site.[23] Third, the tax and the fund applied to land-disposal facilities, such as a landfill or surface impoundment. To the extent that the fund helped insure firms undertaking land disposal, it conflicted with the stated goal of the Hazardous and Solid Waste Amendments (HSWA) of 1984 to minimize the disposal of hazardous wastes in the land. Conversely, to the extent that the HSWA discourages land disposal, it significantly reduces the revenue from this tax on land disposal. Besides, incentives for care are adversely affected by taking liability away from the original owner or operator of the facility.

Finally, the $200 million limit did not allow enough funds to cover likely liability claims. The EPA (1985) estimated that the fund would have less than a 10 percent chance of remaining in positive balance after 100 years. If the $200 million limit were removed, and if the rate were increased over time to account for inflation, the fund would have a 90 percent chance of a positive balance after 100 years.

Faced with a revenue shortfall for a fund that contradicted a national policy to discourage land disposal of hazardous waste, Congress in 1986 decided to repeal the PCLTF and to refund all amounts that had been collected (see U.S. General Accounting Office, 1990).

6. THE SHIFTING OF ENVIRONMENTAL TAX BURDENS

Congress can decide who is legally liable to pay a tax, but it cannot legislate the ultimate distribution of burden. A tax on one good may

---

[23] Environmental Information Ltd. (1993) estimates that 95 percent of hazardous waste-generating firms rely on off-site facilities but that 95.4 percent of hazardous waste volumes were managed on-site in 1989. The implication is that most of this volume is wastewater of relatively few large firms, managed on the premises, usually by deep-well injection, whereas relatively many small firms generate small volumes of other hazardous waste that is sent to disposal facilities.

reverberate through the economy in such a way that other prices are affected. An untaxed good may end up with a higher price, and anyone who buys it bears a burden.[24] This section describes calculations using an input–output model that accounts for some of these indirect effects. Since each industry purchases intermediate inputs that are produced by every other industry, the cost of producing each output depends on the gross-of-tax cost of buying all of its inputs. Section 6.1 describes the model in general terms, and specific assumptions and equations can be found in the Appendix. Section 6.2 calculates price changes attributable to existing environmental taxes.

6.1 The Input–Output Model

Virtually all these environmental taxes apply to the purchase of an intermediate input, such as chemical feedstocks or crude petroleum. Even the tax on gasoline applies to purchases of gasoline by firms that produce other goods. The Superfund also imposes the CET on a measure of corporate income, which is part of value added. All these taxes raise the cost of production. In any particular industry, all firms are assumed to face the same increase in cost. As these firms raise their own output price, their customers may cut back on purchases. Some of these firms may suffer losses in the short run and eventually must cut production or exit the industry. After the dust settles, remaining firms can sell the reduced output at a higher price that just covers the new higher cost of production. Under competitive conditions, with constant returns to scale, the output price rises by exactly the increase in cost.[25] The remaining empirical issue is to determine the extent to which each price rises, that is, each industry's use of taxed inputs and of goods produced using taxed inputs.

The U.S. Department of Commerce (1994, p. 73) provides exactly such a matrix for 479 different industries.[26] A column of this matrix shows, for a particular industry, the amount of each of the 479 outputs that is used as an input. For present purposes, however, fewer categories will suffice. Table 2 shows how the 479 detailed industries are aggregated into 41 categories for this study. The number and name of each industry are

---

[24] For a review of the literature on the ultimate distribution of tax burdens, see Kotlikoff and Summers (1987).

[25] The equilibrium price is also likely to rise in the case of imperfect competition but perhaps not exactly by the amount of the tax (Katz and Rosen, 1985). A monopolist would raise the price by less than the tax.

[26] The most recent complete input–output data are for 1987, but these amounts are scaled to 1990 for each industry using the ratio of gross domestic product in 1990 to that in 1987, available in Yuskavage (1993).

TABLE 2
Aggregation to 41 Industries, Tax Rates, and Price Increases

	Description	Standard industrial classification	Input tax rate (%)^a	CET rate (%)^b	Price increase (%)
1.	Agricultural products	01–02	0.00	0.001	0.28
2.	Agricultural services, forestry, and fishing	07–09	0.00	0.002	0.31
3.	Metal mining	10	0.00	0.025	0.37
4.	Coal mining	11–12	2.53	0.006	0.57
5.	Crude petroleum and natural gas	13	0.69	0.009	0.09
6.	Nonmetallic minerals (except fuels)	14	0.00	0.008	0.29
7.	Construction	15–17	0.00	0.001	0.23
8.	Food and kindred products	20	0.00	0.015	0.25
9.	Tobacco manufacturers	21	0.00	0.056	0.13
10.	Textile mill products	22	0.00	0.006	0.31
11.	Apparel and other textile products	23	0.00	0.006	0.18
12.	Lumber and wood products (except next entry)	24	0.00	0.011	0.27
13.	Wood preserving	2491	0.00	0.013	0.52
14.	Furniture and fixtures	25	0.00	0.006	0.21
15.	Paper and allied products	26	0.00	0.021	0.40
16.	Printing and publishing	27	0.00	0.012	0.21
17.	Inorganic chemicals (2812, −16, −19, −73, −74, −79)	28	0.31	0.099	0.64
18.	Organic chemicals (2813, −65, −69)	28	0.98	0.029	0.66
19.	Chemicals and allied products (except previous two entries)	28	0.00	0.034	0.56
20.	Petroleum refining	2911	6.94	0.151	1.08
21.	Petroleum-related products (except previous entry)	29	0.00	0.105	2.20
22.	Rubber and miscellaneous plastics products	30	0.31	0.004	0.40
23.	Leather and leather products	31	0.00	0.015	0.25
24.	Stone, clay, and glass products	32	0.00	0.014	0.39
25.	Primary metal industries	33	0.00	0.016	0.40
26.	Fabricated metal products	34	0.03	0.008	0.24
27.	Machinery, except electrical	35	0.00	0.018	0.18
28.	Electrical and electronic equipment	36	0.00	0.023	0.20
29.	Motor vehicles and transportation equipment	37	0.39	0.025	0.33

TABLE 2 (Continued)

	Description	Standard industrial classification	Input tax rate (%)[a]	CET rate (%)[b]	Price increase (%)
30.	Instruments and related products	38	0.00	0.009	0.15
31.	Miscellaneous manufacturing	39	0.00	0.016	0.23
32.	Transportation	40–47	1.26	0.007	0.86
33.	Communications	48	0.00	0.030	0.09
34.	Electric, gas, and sanitary services	49	0.00	0.031	0.50
35.	Wholesale trade	50–51	0.00	0.004	0.13
36.	Retail trade	52–59	0.00	0.009	0.11
37.	Finance	60–62, 64, 67	0.00	0.011	0.08
38.	Insurance	63	0.00	0.052	0.09
39.	Real estate	65	0.00	0.001	0.05
40.	Services	70–89	0.00	0.001	0.16
41.	Government enterprises and special industries	91–97	0.00	0.000	0.12

[a] Effective rate of tax on intermediate input of each good, calculated for 1990 as tax liability over the sum of all its intermediate uses.

[b] Effective rate of Corporate Environmental Tax (CET) as a percent of the value added in each industry, calculated for 1990 as CET liabilities over the value added.

listed in the first column, and the Standard Industrial Classification (SIC) is shown in the second column. The aggregation basically represents the two-digit SIC level, with some adjustments. Two-digit levels for most manufacturing industries are retained (SIC 20–39), but wood preserving is separated from other lumber and wood products (because wood preserving is involved in a number of contaminated sites), and petroleum refining is separated from other petroleum-related products. Chemicals are divided into three categories that are taxed at different rates (taxed organic chemicals, taxed inorganic chemicals, and untaxed chemicals). Then nonmanufacturing industries are collapsed into fewer categories. Just two industries are used to represent agriculture, and just one industry is used for each of construction, transportation, wholesale trade, retail trade, finance, and services.

The whole matrix is not shown here, but the data confirm general expectations. The output of "crude petroleum and natural gas" (item 5 in Table 2) is a major input to "petroleum refining" (item 20), whereas the output of refined petroleum is a major input to "petroleum-related products" (item 21) and "transportation" (item 32). These petroleum products are also important inputs to "organic chemicals" (item 18, sometimes called petrochemicals). Both organic and inorganic chemicals (item 17) are inputs to the other (untaxed) chemical industry (item 19), and they are also major inputs to "textile mill products" (item 10) and to "wood preserving" (item 13).

The third column of Table 2 shows how each environmental tax in Table 1 is converted into an effective rate of tax on one of the intermediate inputs of the model.[27] In general, each effective tax rate is calculated as the observed amount of tax divided by the tax base (which most often is the total intermediate use of that input).[28] Coal, for example, is purchased primarily by the electric utilities industry (item 34 in Table 2) but also to some degree by primary metals (item 25) and other industries. Final demand by consumers is virtually nil. Thus, the observed tax on coal is divided by total intermediate use of coal to obtain the 2.53 percent tax rate shown in Table 2. Similarly, the petroleum tax applied to all purchases of crude petroleum. Unfortunately, even the most detailed input–output data employ only one industry for "crude petroleum and natural gas" (item 5), and its "output" is purchased both by refineries and by utilities. However, virtually all the crude oil is purchased by refineries (item 20), whereas the natural gas is purchased by gas distribution utilities (item 34). Therefore, in the model, the tax is applied not to all intermediate use of output (item 5), but only to the intermediate use of item 5 by item 20. The effective rate of tax for both Superfund and the OSLTF is 0.69 percent. This rate matches closely the statutory tax rate ($0.147 per barrel) divided by the average price of oil (about $20 per barrel).

Chemical feedstock taxes apply at different rates on various chemicals used by any industry. Several of the 479 industries that produce taxed inorganic chemicals are aggregated into one industry (item 17), where the observed tax is divided by total intermediate use to obtain an effective tax rate of 0.31 percent. Some organic chemicals (item 18) are taxed as chemical feedstocks under the Superfund, and some are taxed as ozone-depleting chemicals. The total of these two taxes divided by total use of taxed organic chemicals yields the effective tax rate of 0.98 percent.

Many individual chemical products are known to be taxed at rates that approach 2 percent of their price (see Dougherty and Gilson, 1994, pp. 4-2 to 4-6). Even with 479 industries, however, the input–output matrix

---

[27] These effective tax rates represent the statutory incidence, that is, the tax that is collected on each of these inputs. These tax rates are used here to calculate the economic incidence, that is, the increase in the 41 equilibrium output prices.

[28] The effective tax rates in Table 2 are calculated from tax amounts for 1990 because the quantities in the input–output matrix are for 1990.

does not separately identify these individual products. Some of the 479 industries produced only untaxed chemicals, and these were aggregated into industry (item 19), but most of the chemical industries on this list produced both taxed and untaxed chemicals. Thus, the categories for inorganic chemicals (item 17) and organic chemicals (item 18) necessarily include some untaxed chemicals. Each industry produces one "output" in the model, so this procedure effectively averages over the taxed and untaxed goods within an industry and applies a single effective tax rate to that "output."

Other taxes do not distinguish between intermediate and final purchases, so the effective rate is calculated as the observed tax over total output. The model then applies this rate to all intermediate purchases to calculate the effect on production costs in other industries. For example, the sum of all taxes on motor fuels is divided by total output of "refined petroleum" (item 20) to obtain the effective tax rate of 6.94 percent shown in Table 2. The tax on tires is divided by all output of "rubber and miscellaneous plastics products" (item 22) to get the 0.31 percent rate; the tax on pistols and revolvers is divided by all "fabricated metal products" (item 26) for the 0.03 percent rate; taxes on trucks and gas guzzlers are divided by total output of "motor vehicles and transportation equipment" (item 29) to get the 0.39 percent rate; and observed taxes on transportation of persons and property are divided by total output of "transportation" (item 32) for the 1.26 percent rate.

Finally, the fourth column of Table 2 shows the effective rate of the CET. The CET actually applies to part of profits for each firm, namely the "modified" AMTI over $2 million. A more complicated general equilibrium model might be able to calculate the effect of this tax on the wage rate and the interest rate—and thus the extent to which the burden is passed backward onto labor and capital (see, for example, Shoven and Whalley, 1984.) Instead, this simpler model assumes fixed economy-wide rates of return to labor and capital and, therefore, fixed value added in each industry. The effective tax rate for each industry is calculated as the CET liability divided by the value added in that industry. This effective rate then represents the percent increase in value added that is required for each industry: labor and capital must produce enough to cover this tax as well as their returns. These higher costs are reflected in output prices and in the cost to other industries of buying those outputs as intermediate inputs. The ultimate burden is therefore passed forward onto consumers.

The Appendix describes equations for each of the 41 industries that say that the value of output (price times quantity) is equal to the cost of all the inputs. In long-run equilibrium, no firm receives excess profits.

The cost side includes the price and amount of each intermediate input and the value added. The prices of nine intermediate inputs are increased by the tax rates in the third column of Table 2, and the value added is increased by the tax rates in the fourth column. Thus, the 41 equations all involve the 41 prices as well as other variables. Since these equations are linear, matrix algebra is used to solve for the 41 prices as functions of the other variables (intermediate inputs, tax rates, and value added).

In other words, a simultaneous solution for all prices accounts for how each price depends on all other prices of goods that may be used as inputs. This procedure considers not only taxes on the nine taxed intermediate goods, but also the increased cost of some other intermediate inputs that may themselves be produced using one or more of the nine taxed inputs.

6.2 Results

The percent price increase for each of the 41 outputs is shown in the last column of Table 2. Even with these nine separate environmental taxes, only two output prices are affected by more than 1 percent. The price of refined petroleum (item 20) rises by 1.08 percent, primarily because of the tax on input of crude oil (item 5). The price of petroleum-related products (item 21) rises by 2.20 percent because of the increased price of refined petroleum, plus the additional tax on refined petroleum, plus the additional tax on the input of organic chemicals (item 18).

The price increase for each good in Table 2 reflects the cost of inputs, not additional tax on the output. Thus, the 0.86 percent increase in the price of transportation (item 32) reflects not the tax on the output of the transportation industry, but increased costs of production from taxes on purchases of refined petroleum (item 20) and transportation equipment (item 29). The gross-of-tax price of transportation then increases by the 0.86 percent price increase and the 1.26 percent tax, a factor of $(1.0086)(1.0126) = 1.0213$ (a gross increase of 2.13 percent).

An interesting general result in Table 2 is the extent to which every price rises. Every industry uses some transportation and some electricity that are produced using taxed fuels that are produced using taxed crude petroleum. Thus, Congress is not able to target the burden of particular taxes on particular industries. Another striking result in Table 2 is the extent of increases in the prices of untaxed goods. The price of agricultural output rises by 0.3 percent, for example, in part because that industry uses fertilizer made from taxed organic chemicals. Textile prices rise 0.3 percent because of the use of agricultural output, chemicals, transportation, and electricity. Primary metals prices rise 0.4 percent because of use of coal, chemicals, electricity, and transportation. Other goods are then produced using primary metals.

These tax rates and results are shown graphically in Figure 1. The long solid bars for a few industries are the tax rates, and the many short open bars for all industries are the percent increases in price. The shifting of burdens looks like mowing the tall weeds down to grass.

Similar diffuse burdens would result from incentive-based taxes on smokestack emissions or hazardous waste, since these would be paid by industries that produce goods used by other industries. The spreading of burden is not itself a problem. It just means that legislated tax policy cannot achieve the fairness objective of placing burden on a particular industry.

7. CONCLUSION

Why have separate environmental taxes? A separate tax would be needed to use incentives to discourage an activity with a negative externality that harms the environment. A good example would be a tax on a polluting emission itself rather than on a commodity like gasoline, which is only weakly correlated with emissions. But attempts to target taxes on narrowly defined behaviors create costs of measurement, administration, and compliance. Perhaps for these reasons, as well as for political reasons, Congress prefers to control emissions and other environmentally damaging activities directly, through command and control regulations such as emission standards on all new vehicles.

Many current taxes might be thought to have environmental effects, but none of them is a good example of an incentive-based tax. Better examples might be proposed. The current tax on gasoline is not tied to emissions of carbon monoxide or hydrocarbons, but vehicle emission taxes are now becoming feasible (Harrington, Walls, and McConnell, 1994). For another example, a tax on the carbon content of each fuel would indeed be tied directly to emissions of carbon dioxide that cause global warming. For a final example, the Clean Air Act of 1990 currently hands out sulfur dioxide permits in proportion to past emissions, but it could be converted to a revenue-raising instrument by selling the permits or by taxing those emissions.

Instead, policymakers use separate taxes to finance the cleanup of each environmental problem while collecting from the industry thought to be responsible. But these attempts to target taxes on narrow industries also create substantial costs of administration and compliance. Each separate tax has a fixed cost associated with filling out forms and ensuring compliance. Thus, the compliance cost per dollar of revenue starts

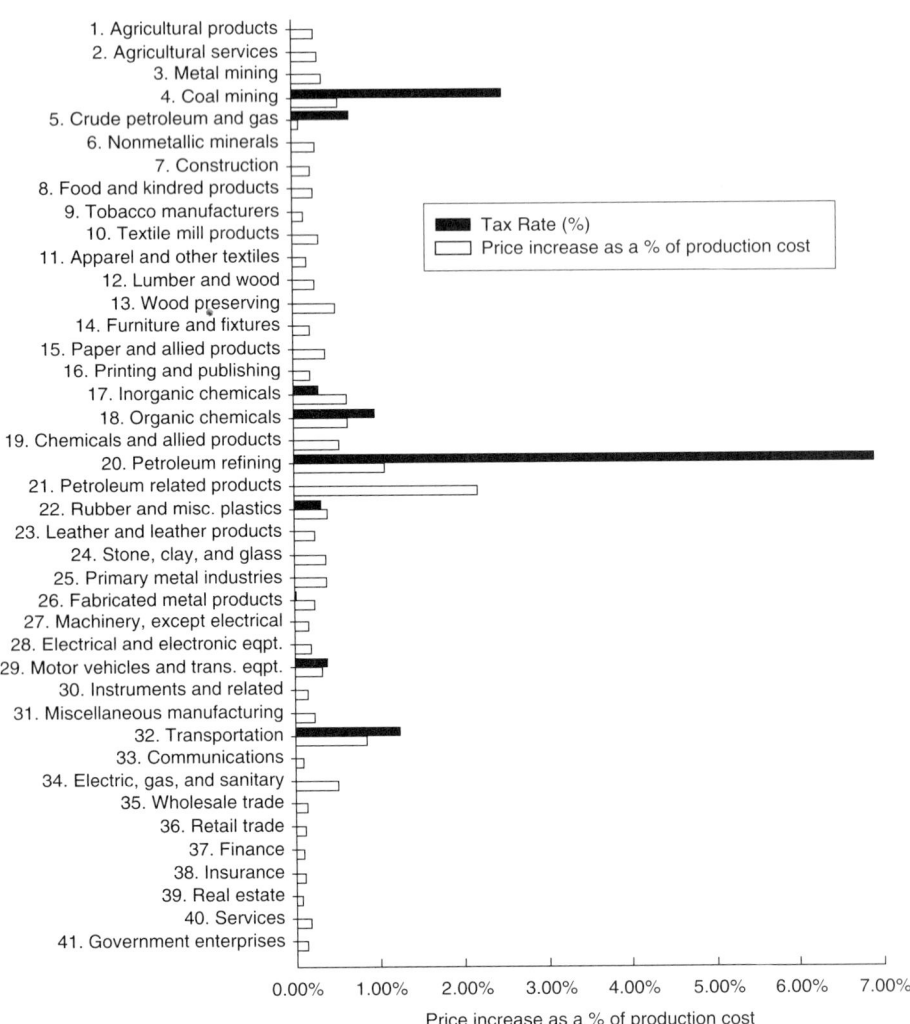

FIGURE 1. *Price increase for each final output, with current environmental taxes.*

out high, whereas the tax rate and revenue are low. Each tax exhibits economies of scale, as an increase in the rate can acquire additional revenue without filling out more forms. A problem, then, is that each separate environmental tax requires its own forms, imposes a very low rate, and collects very little revenue.

Finally, these separate taxes and compliance costs do not achieve the goal of targeting burdens on particular industries. Using an input–output model of the U.S. economy, this paper shows how the burden of environmental taxes is distributed among all industries. Thus, the high administrative and compliance costs of having many separate environmental taxes are achieving neither targeted incentives nor targeted burdens. A tiny 0.1 percent increase in broad-based income taxes would collect the same revenue, have the same diffuse distributional effects, and create virtually none of the additional administrative and compliance costs.

APPENDIX: INPUT–OUTPUT ANALYSIS

The ultimate incidence or burdens on consumers depends on the impact of each tax on the price of each output. In addition, if some industries use taxed commodities as intermediate inputs, then the burden is further shifted to the consumers of those outputs. Under constant returns to scale and perfect competition, all increases in costs are passed to consumers through higher prices. The burden is not only on consumers of taxed goods, such as chemicals and petroleum, but also on consumers of goods produced using taxed chemicals and petroleum. These price effects can be estimated using input–output analysis as developed early in the 1950s by Wassily Leontief (see Leontief, 1986) in a model like that of Probst et al. (1995).

A.1 Assumptions

Several important assumptions are necessary for the model. First, the demand for every industry's output is assumed to be large enough to accommodate plenty of firms that each achieve a scale where costs are minimized. Entry barriers do not reduce the number of firms or the extent of competition. Since any change in output can be met by changes in the number of firms, all operating at minimum cost, the industry is competitive, and marginal cost is constant. No firm makes abnormal profits, in the long run, after all prices and outputs have adjusted. The reasonableness of this assumption can be checked by looking at four-firm concentration ratios, the percent of each industry output that is produced by the largest four firms in the industry.[29] When this ratio is less than half, Scherer (1979) concludes that the industry is adequately competitive. These ratios show that perfect competition and constant costs are adequate approximations of reality.[30]

Second, input coefficients are assumed fixed, so each output must be produced using unchanged proportions of each intermediate input and the value added. When one input price rises, producers cannot switch and use more of a different input. The model thus accounts for first-order effects on the price of an output that is produced using a mix of intermediate inputs but not second-order effects on changes in the mix. Therefore, calculated tax revenue is only an approximation. This assumption captures the effect on output price, so producers may decrease output by decreasing all inputs, but it misses the possibility that producers might switch from a taxed input to an untaxed input.

Third, consider the choice of assumption about international trade. If each good were traded, and if the imported good were a perfect substitute for the domestically produced good, then any attempted change in the price of the domestic good would induce purchasers to switch entirely to the foreign good. The price of each good in the United States would be completely determined by world markets and would not be affected by any domestic tax policy. At the opposite extreme, if the economy were closed, then the domestic price of each good could be determined from information on the costs of production (as in this model). But this other extreme is too restrictive. Instead, the model is still valid under the less restrictive assumption that each foreign good is an imperfect substitute for the corresponding domestic good.[31] As long as the two goods are not identical, then an increase in the price of the domestic good may induce purchasers to substitute incompletely toward the foreign good. This possibility makes the demand for the domestic good more elastic, but in this model price is independent of the shape of the demand curve. The important point here is that the price of the domestic good is still determined by the location of the cost curve.

---

[29] These concentration ratios can be found in U.S. Department of Commerce (1980). Tax incidence with imperfect competition is analyzed by Katz and Rosen (1985).

[30] More discussion on this point can be found in Fullerton and Tsang (1993) and Probst, Fullerton, Litan, and Portney (1995).

[31] This assumption follows Armington (1969). A Ford car is not the same as a Volvo or a Mercedes, and consumers can substitute between them in a way that depends on their relative prices. If environmental taxes on inputs raise domestic car output prices, then some consumers may switch to foreign cars. The demand for American cars may fall, but not to zero. Imperfect substitutability is irrelevant when imports are subject to the same taxes as domestic goods.

Finally, some indirect effects are ignored. The model is not a general equilibrium model with multiple factors of production and consumer groups with demands for each final output. Thus, it does not account for changes in wages or the rate of return. For present purposes, the simpler model provides meaningful and helpful results while avoiding excessive complications.

A.2 Equations

Assume that the national economy can be aggregated into n industries and a sector of final demands that includes household and government purchases. The dollar values of transactions among sectors can be presented in the following transactions matrix S:

$$S = \begin{bmatrix} x_{11}p_1 & x_{12}p_1 & \cdots & x_{1n}p_1 & d_1p_1 \\ x_{21}p_2 & x_{22}p_2 & \cdots & x_{2n}p_2 & d_2p_2 \\ \vdots & \vdots & \vdots & \vdots & \vdots \\ x_{n1}p_n & x_{n2}p_n & \cdots & x_{nn}p_n & d_np_n \\ v_1 & v_2 & \cdots & v_n & \end{bmatrix} \qquad (1)$$

where p_i represents the price per unit of product i; d_i is the final demand for output i; and v_i represents the value added of the ith industry. Each row shows the intermediate and final uses of an input, and each column shows the intermediate and factor inputs of an industry. For example, x_{21} is the physical quantity of the output from industry 2 that is used by industry 1. With no loss in generality, the unit price convention defines the physical unit of each commodity as the amount that sells for $1. Since all prices are one, dollar volume in equation (1) can be used to derive the input coefficients. Let x_j be the sum of all demands in row j, a measure of total output. Then define a_{ij} as the "input coefficient," the input of the ith good as a fraction of total output of industry j:

$$a_{ij} = x_{ij}/x_j, \qquad (2)$$

where

$$x_j = \sum_{i=1}^{n} x_{ji} + d_j.$$

These input coefficients are assumed constant. This assumption is useful and appropriate for calculating first-order effects on the cost of output from variations in the cost of different inputs, as done here, but it does not account for second-order effects, such as changes in the mix of inputs. These second-order effects would be necessary to estimate efficiency effects from tax distortions or to estimate tax revenue after adjustments in behavior.

As long as profits are included in the value added, the sum of all inputs plus value-added is equal to the value of gross output. Also, the sum of all intermediate and final uses is equal to the value of gross output. Thus each column sum of matrix (1) is equal to the corresponding row sum:

$$
\begin{aligned}
x_{11}p_1 + x_{21}p_2 + \cdots + x_{n1}p_n + v_1 &= x_1 p_1, \\
x_{12}p_1 + x_{22}p_2 + \cdots + x_{n2}p_n + v_2 &= x_2 p_2, \\
\vdots \quad \vdots \quad \cdots \quad \vdots \quad \vdots & \\
x_{1n}p_1 - x_{2n}p_2 + \cdots + x_{nn}p_n + v_n &= x_n p_n.
\end{aligned}
\tag{3}
$$

Each of these equations is divided by total output of that industry x_i and then rearranged and reexpressed using the input coefficients to find

$$
\begin{aligned}
(1 - a_{11})p_1 - a_{21}p_2 - \cdots - a_{n1}p_n &= v_1/x_1, \\
- a_{12}p_1 + (1 - a_{22})p_2 - \cdots - a_{n2}p_n &= v_2/x_2, \\
\vdots \quad \vdots \quad \cdots \quad \vdots & \\
- a_{1n}p_1 - a_{2n}p_2 - \cdots + (1 - a_{nn}p_n) &= v_n/x_n.
\end{aligned}
\tag{4}
$$

Using matrix algebra, these equations can then be represented by

$$(I - A')P = V, \tag{5}$$

where

$$
A = \begin{bmatrix} a_{11} & a_{12} & \cdots & a_{1n} \\ a_{21} & a_{22} & \cdots & a_{2n} \\ \vdots & \vdots & \cdots & \vdots \\ a_{n1} & a_{n2} & \cdots & a_{nn} \end{bmatrix}, \quad P = \begin{bmatrix} p_1 \\ p_2 \\ \vdots \\ p_n \end{bmatrix}, \quad V = \begin{bmatrix} v_1/x_1 \\ v_2/x_2 \\ \vdots \\ v_n/x_n \end{bmatrix},
$$

and where I is the identity matrix. If $(I - A')$ is nonsingular, the price vector can be derived as follows:

$$P = (I - A')^{-1} V. \tag{6}$$

With the Armington (1969) assumption, each foreign good is not a perfect substitute for the corresponding domestic good. Since prices are not already set by international trade, equation (6) can be used to calculate the impact of alternative policies on the price vector.

Tax rates on nine intermediate inputs (such as petroleum and chemical feedstocks) are shown in Table 2. If each intermediate input has its own tax rate (regardless of where it is used), then equation (3) can be expressed as follows:

$$x_{11}p_1(1 + t_1) + x_{21}p_2(1 + t_2) + \cdots + x_{n1}p_n(1 + t_n) + v_1 = x_1p_1,$$
$$x_{12}p_1(1 + t_1) + x_{22}p_2(1 + t_2) + \cdots + x_{n2}p_n(1 + t_n) + v_2 = x_2p_2, \quad (7)$$
$$\vdots \qquad \vdots \qquad \cdots \qquad \vdots \qquad \vdots \qquad \vdots$$
$$x_{1n}p_1(1 + t_1) + x_{2n}p_2(1 + t_2) + \cdots + x_{nn}p_n(1 + t_n) + v_n = x_np_n.$$

Using steps similar to those used in deriving equations (3)–(6), then

$$\mathbf{P} = (\mathbf{I} - \mathbf{A}'\mathbf{T}_I)^{-1}\mathbf{V}, \quad (8)$$

where

$$\mathbf{T}_I = \begin{bmatrix} 1 + t_1 & 0 & 0 & 0 \\ 0 & 1 + t_2 & 0 & 0 \\ 0 & 0 & \cdots & 0 \\ 0 & 0 & 0 & 1 + t_n \end{bmatrix}.$$

Finally, the CET is added to the model. If all industries face the same rate of CET, say t, and the AMTI of each industry is a fraction α_i of the value added of the ith industry, then

$$\mathbf{P} = (\mathbf{I} - \mathbf{A}'\mathbf{T}_I)^{-1}\mathbf{T}_C\mathbf{V}, \quad (9)$$

where

$$\mathbf{T}_C = \begin{bmatrix} 1 + t \times \alpha_1 & 0 & 0 & 0 \\ 0 & 1 + t \times \alpha_2 & 0 & 0 \\ 0 & 0 & \cdots & 0 \\ 0 & 0 & 0 & 1 + t \times \alpha_n \end{bmatrix}.$$

One problem in using the 1987 benchmark input–output data is that the transactions are subdivided into a "make-matrix" ($\mathbf{M}_{I \times C}$), which shows how much each industry makes of each commodity, and a use-matrix ($\mathbf{U}_{C \times I}$), which shows how much of each commodity is used by each industry. To derive the industry-by-industry transactions matrix ($\mathbf{S}_{I \times I}$), divide each entry of $\mathbf{M}_{I \times C}$ by its column sum and multiply:

$$\mathbf{S}_{I \times I} = \mathbf{M}_{I \times C} \times \mathbf{U}_{C \times I}. \tag{10}$$

Including another row and column for the value added and final demand generates the $\mathbf{S}$ matrix of equation (1). The next step is to derive a_{ij} from the units convention and equation (2).

Data for $\mathbf{T}_I$ and $\mathbf{T}_C$ are shown in Table 2. For example, petroleum tax liability for 1990 is divided by intermediate use of crude petroleum by refineries to obtain t_5 of $\mathbf{T}_I$. Similarly, the ratio of tax liability for each chemical divided by total intermediate uses of that chemical provides the t_i for each chemical in $\mathbf{T}_I$. The fourth column of Table 2 provides the source for $\mathbf{T}_C$ in 1990.

REFERENCES

Alberini, Anna, David Edelstein, Winston Harrington, and Virginia D. McConnell (1994). "Reducing Emissions from Old Cars: The Economics of the Delaware Vehicle Retirement Program." Discussion Paper no. 94-27, Washington, DC: Resources for the Future.

Armington, Paul S. (1969). "A Theory of Demand for Products Distinguished by Place of Production." *International Monetary Fund Staff Papers* 16:159–176.

Barthold, Thomas A. (1994). "Issues in the Design of Environmental Excise Taxes." *Journal of Economic Perspectives* 8(no. 1, Winter): 133–151.

Baumol, William J., and Wallace E. Oates (1988). *The Theory of Environmental Policy.* New York: Cambridge University Press.

Bohm, Peter (1981). *Deposit-Refund Systems.* Baltimore: The Johns Hopkins University Press, for Resources for the Future.

———, and Clifford S. Russell (1985). "Comparative Analysis of Alternative Policy Instruments." In *Handbook of Natural Resource and Energy Economics,* Vol. I, Allen V. Kneese and James L. Sweeney (eds.). Amsterdam: North Holland.

Burmich, Pam (1989). "The Air Pollution–Transportation Linkage." Sacramento, CA: State of California Air Resources Board, Office of Strategic Planning.

Carlson, J. Lon, and Charles W. Bausell, Jr. (1987). "Financing Superfund: An Evaluation of Alternative Tax Mechanisms." *Natural Resources Journal* 27 (Winter):103–122.

Commerce Clearing House, Inc. (1995). *1995 U.S. Excise Tax Guide.* Chicago.

Davie, Bruce F. (1993). "Excise Taxes, Fiscal Year 1992." *Statistics of Income Bulletin* 13(no. 2, Fall). Washington, DC: Internal Revenue Service, U.S. Treasury Department.

———(1995). "Border Adjustments for Environmental Excise Taxes: The U.S. Experience." Washington, DC: Office of Tax Analysis, U.S. Treasury Department.

Dougherty, Charlotte P., and Elizabeth S. Gilson (1994). "Economic Impacts of

Superfund Taxes." February. Washington, DC: Industrial Economics Inc., for the U.S. Environmental Protection Agency.
Environmental Information Ltd. (1993). *Interdependence in the Management of Hazardous Waste.* Minneapolis, MN.
Fullerton, Don, and Thomas C. Kinnaman (1995). "Garbage, Recycling, and Illicit Burning or Dumping," *Journal of Environmental Economics and Management* 29(July):78–91.
———, and Seng-Su Tsang (1993). "Environmental Costs Paid by the Polluter or the Beneficiary: The Case of CERCLA and Superfund." NBER Working Paper no. 4418, Cambridge, MA.
Harrington, Winston, Margaret A. Walls, and Virginia McConnell (1994). "Shifting Gears: New Directions for Cars and Clean Air." Discussion Paper no. 94-26-REV. Washington, DC: Resources for the Future.
Katz, Michael L., and Harvey S. Rosen (1985). "Tax Analysis in an Oligopoly Model." *Public Finance Quarterly* 13(no. 1, January):3–19.
Kotlikoff, Laurence J., and Lawrence H. Summers (1987). "Tax Incidence." In *Handbook of Public Economics,* Vol. 2, Alan Auerbach and Martin Felstein (eds.). Amsterdam: Elsevier Science Publishers.
Leontief, Wassily (1986). *Input-Output Economics,* 2nd ed., New York: Oxford University Press.
Lyon, Andrew B. (1991). "The Alternative Minimum Tax: Equity, Efficiency, and Incentive Effects." In *Economic Effects of the Corporate Alternative Minimum Tax.* Washington, DC: American Council for Capital Formation.
McNiel, Douglas W., and Andrew W. Foshee (1988). "Superfund Financing Alternatives." *Policy Studies Review* 7(no. 4, Summer):751–760.
Merrill, Peter R., and Ada S. Rousso (1991). "Federal Environmental Taxation." In *Proceedings of the Eighty-Third Annual Conference of the National Tax Association,* November 1990, San Francisco, CA.
Pigou, Arthur C. (1932). *The Economics of Welfare,* 4th ed. London, UK: MacMillan and Co.
Plamondon and Associates, Inc. (1993). *GST Compliance Costs for Small Business in Canada.* Canadian Tax Executive Institute.
Poterba, James M., and Julio J. Rotemberg (1995). "Environmental Taxes on Intermediate and Final Goods When Both Can Be Imported." *International Tax and Public Finance* 2(August):221–228.
Price Waterhouse (1992). "Evaluation of Superfund Financing Options." Washington, DC.
Probst, Katherine N., Don Fullerton, Robert E. Litan, and Paul R. Portney (1995). *Footing the Bill for Superfund Cleanups: Who Pays and How?* Washington DC: The Brookings Institution and Resources for the Future.
Sandford, Cedric, Michael Godwin, and Peter Hardwick (1989). *Administrative and Compliance Costs of Taxation.* Bath, UK: Fiscal Publications.
Scherer, F. M. (1979). *Industrial Market Structure and Economic Performance,* 2nd ed. Chicago: Rand McNally College Publishing Company.
Shoven, John B., and John Whalley (1984). "Applied General Equilibrium Models of Taxation and International Trade: An Introduction and Survey." *Journal of Economic Literature* 22(September):1007–1051.
Sierra Research (1994). "Analysis of the Effectiveness and Cost-Effectiveness of Remote Sensing Devices." Report no. SR94-05-05, prepared for the U.S. Environmental Protection Agency. Sacramento, CA: Sierra Research.

Slemrod, Joel, and Marsha Blumenthal (1993). *The Income Tax Compliance Cost of Big Business*. Washington, DC: Tax Foundation.
———and Nikki Sorum (1984). "The Compliance Cost of the U.S. Individual Income Tax System." *National Tax Journal* 37(December):461–474.
U.S. Department of Commerce (1980). "Concentration Ratios in Manufacturing." In *Census of Manufacturers*. Washington, DC: Bureau of Census.
———(1994). "Benchmark Input-Output Accounts for the U.S. Economy, 1987. In *Survey of Current Business*, vol. 74, April. Washington, DC: Bureau of Economic Analysis.
U.S. Environmental Protection Agency (1985). "Report to the Congress of the United States on the Post-Closure Liability Trust Fund Under Section 301(a) (2) (ii) of the Comprehensive Environmental Response, Compensation and Liability Act of 1980." Washington, DC: Office of Solid Waste.
U.S. General Accounting Office (1990). *Hazardous Waste: Funding of Postclosure Liabilities Remains Uncertain*. GAO/RCED-90-64. Washington, DC.
Walls, Margaret, and Jean Hanson (1995). "Measuring the Incidence of an Environmental Tax Shift: The Case of Motor Vehicle Emissions Taxes." Washington, DC: Resources for the Future.
Yuskavage, Robert E. (1993). "Gross Product by Industry, 1988–91." In *Survey of Current Business*, vol. 73, November, pp. 33–44. Washington, DC: Bureau of Economic Analysis.

THE EFFECTS OF TAX REFORM ON PRICES AND ASSET VALUES

Robert E. Hall
Stanford University and NBER

EXECUTIVE SUMMARY

All forms of consumption taxes have the same basic, desirable effect on the economy—they eliminate the distortion present in an income tax between current and future consumption. But different ways of administering consumption taxes have different effects in the long run and especially during the transition. Sales taxes and value-added taxes require a one-time increase in the price level, a shock that the Hall–Rabushka and personal consumption taxes avoid. The basis value-added tax (VAT) requires a one-time appreciation of the dollar, a shock that other consumption taxes avoid. Generally, consumption taxes would impose a new tax on the rental value of owner-occupied housing, which might have a small adverse net effect on housing. This effect could be offset by a personal housing deduction. The present paper also discusses effects on interest rates, bonds, equities, human capital, and retirement saving.

This paper was prepared for the 1995 National Bureau of Economic Research Conference on Tax Policy and the Economy, Washington, D.C., November 7. I am grateful to E. Cary Brown for early counseling in these matters, to David Bradford for helpful discussions over the past two decades, and to James Poterba and Dale Jorgenson for comments on the earlier draft. All remaining errors are mine.

1. INTRODUCTION

Tax reform is concentrating more and more on consumption taxes. The wedge of the income tax raises the price of later consumption relative to the price of current consumption. A basic goal of consumption taxation is to remove that wedge. The rationale is deep and general—in an intertemporal economy, capital is an intermediate product, and it is undesirable to tax intermediate products at all.

A tax reform that replaces an income tax with a consumption tax has a key intertemporal effect. Under an income tax at rate τ, the relative price of consumption this year is distorted by the factor $(1 - \tau)^i$ relative to consumption i years from now. The cheapening of current consumption relative to future consumption caused by an income tax is the source of its disincentive for saving. Under a consumption tax, there is no distortion at all between present and future consumption. The incentive to save is at its efficient level.

There are many ways to set up a consumption tax, but all of them have the same fundamental effect on the economy. The only distortion present under a consumption tax is between the household's internal use of time and time spent in the market. At the most basic level, different forms of consumption taxes cannot be judged by their effects on relative prices. Still, it is important to understand the various ways that value-added taxes, sales taxes, and personal consumption taxes differ. Relative prices differ among these consumption taxes because under some tax systems, prices and wages are quoted before taxes and under others, after taxes. The immediate effects of tax reform can differ because of wage rigidity and because there are one-time wealth effects associated with the before- and after-tax distinction.

To give some organization to the discussion, I will proceed in the following way. I start by describing the various consumption tax systems that are under consideration. These are three variants of the value-added tax, the sales tax, and the personal consumption tax. Then I lay out the basic effects of the taxes on atemporal relative prices in an open economy and draw certain conclusions about the transition. Next, I consider the implications of nominal wage rigidity in order to describe the effects of tax reform on nominal prices and the value of nominal debt. I move on to the more difficult territory of intertemporal effects, particularly interest rates. I then consider the effects of tax reform on housing and human capital. Finally, I examine the key transition issue of the possible double taxation of assets accumulated under an income tax used to finance consumption under a consumption tax.

2. TAXES CONSIDERED

A *value-added tax* (VAT) is a tax on firms on the difference between total revenue and purchases of intermediate products from other firms. Purchases of capital goods are counted as intermediate products. I will assume that firms quote their prices inclusive of the VAT. With respect to foreign trade, the VAT may be on an origin or destination basis. The *origin-basis VAT* includes revenue from foreign sales in the base and permits deductions for purchases of intermediate products from foreign sources. The *destination-basis VAT* excludes exports and imports, or, equivalently, imposes an import duty at the VAT rate and pays a rebate on exports. Finally, the *Hall–Rabushka VAT* (Hall and Rabushka, 1995) is a variant of the origin-basis VAT in which the firm deducts the wages that it pays, and there is a personal wage tax at the VAT rate. The motivation for this complication is that it permits easy administration of an exemption in order to make the VAT progressive. The Hall–Rabushka proposal is usually called the flat tax, although it really has two brackets, one at zero and the other at a single positive rate. Many popular discussions of the flat tax do not refer to the Hall-Rabushka proposal and may not even refer to consumption taxes.

A *consumption sales tax* is a tax imposed on sellers of consumption goods at the point where they go into the hands of final consumers. Again, I assume that firms quote prices inclusive of tax. I will also assume that the tax is on the destination basis—it is imposed on imported consumption goods, and all exported goods are free from tax.

A *personal consumption tax* measures consumption at the household level on a cash-flow basis. It is a personal income tax with an unlimited deduction for saving. The Nunn–Domenici U.S. tax includes a personal consumption tax as well as an 11 percent VAT.

With respect to houses, I will assume that the VATs and the sales tax are imposed on the sellers of new houses and that the purchase of a new house is treated as consumption under a personal consumption tax. The latter assumption is probably not realistic, but it does not seem worthwhile to track down the complexities in the way that housing would actually be handled under a personal consumption tax.

All the taxes thus far described are consumption taxes. The tax base for the destination VAT, the consumption sales tax, and the personal consumption tax is literally consumption as measured in the national income accounts, except that housing is treated as a consumer durable. The tax base for the origin VAT differs by the amount of the trade surplus. But, since the present discounted value of the trade surplus must be the net indebtedness of the United States to the rest of the world, which was determined by history, the origin VAT differs from a consumption tax only by a lump sum.

3. BASIC ATEMPORAL EFFECTS

To explain the basic effects, I will make the simplifying assumption that there is only one kind of output. Absent taxes, all types of output would have the same price. As numeraire, I will take the consumption good after the VAT or sales tax but before the personal tax. I assume competition in all markets. I denote the marginal product of labor by λ. The prices I consider are the following:

1. the wage paid by the firm;
2. the wage received by the worker;
3. the price of traded goods paid by the export customer or received by the import supplier;
4. the price of investment goods received by the seller;
5. the value of investment goods to the owner, net of tax; and
6. the value of housing to the owner, net of tax.

Table 1 shows the effects on these relative prices of the various taxes.

4. TRANSITION ISSUES INFERRED FROM EFFECTS ON RELATIVE PRICES

As I noted in Section 1, the immediate effects of a move to a consumption tax involve not only the relative price effects displayed in Table 1, but also issues of wage rigidity and changes in interest rates. Still, some important inferences follow from Table 1.

First, under either the destination or origin VATs or under the sales tax, the real product wage must fall by the amount of the tax. Under the existing income tax, wages are set on a pretax basis, whereas under the VATs or sales tax, wages are set on an after-tax basis. Most of the issues associated with the lowering of the real product wage have to do with wage rigidity, so I will defer further discussion of this point until Section 5.

Second, under the destination-basis VAT or under the sales tax, the price of traded goods falls below the price of consumption goods by the amount of the tax. These taxes are hugely attractive to politicians because the export subsidy and import tax are thought to improve some-

TABLE 1
Prices Relative to Domestic Consumption Goods

	Destination-basis VAT	Origin-basis VAT	Consumption sales tax	Hall–Rabushka	Personal consumption tax	Personal income tax
Cost of labor to firm	$(1-t)\lambda$	$(1-t)\lambda$	$(1-t)\lambda$	λ	λ	λ
note	a	a	a	b	b	b
Benefit of work to worker	$(1-t)\lambda$	$(1-t)\lambda$	$(1-t)\lambda$	$(1-t)\lambda$	$(1-t)\lambda$	$(1-t)\lambda$
note	c,d	c,d	c,d	d,e	d,e	d,e
Traded goods	$1-t$	1	$1-t$	1	1	1
note	f	f	g	g	g	
Price received by seller of investment goods	1	1	$1-t$	1	1	1
note	h	h	i	h	h	h
Value of investment goods to owner	$1-t$	$1-t$	$1-t$	$1-t$	$1-t$	1
note	j	j	k	j	j	l
Houses	1	1	1	1	1	1
note	m	m	m	m	m	m

[a] For the two VATs and the sales tax, the goods–work wedge occurs within the firm. The equilibrium wage at zero profit is equal to the net after-tax selling price ($-t$) multiplied by the marginal product of labor λ.

[b] For the three taxes where the wage component is collected at the personal level, there is no tax wedge at the firm level.

[c] For the two VATs and the sales tax, the wage paid and the wage received are the same.

[d] Hence, all six taxes drive the same wedge between the benefit of working and the price of consumption goods. The wedge is the inescapable inefficiency of taxation when it is impossible to tax the consumption of time at home.

[e] For the three taxes where the wage component is collected at the personal level, there is no tax wedge at that level.

[f] The destination VAT and the sales tax raise the price of consumption goods above traded goods because the tax is levied on imports and rebated on exports.

[g] Consumption goods and traded goods have the same price for taxes without border adjustments.

[h] For the VATs, including Hall–Rabushka, purchasers pay the same price for investment goods as for consumption goods; they receive the tax incentive for investment through a deduction against their own taxes. The personal consumption tax provides the incentive on the saving rather than the investment side, so it has equal prices for consumption and investment. Finally, the personal income tax does not have an incentive, so it, too, keeps the prices the same.

[i] Under the consumption sales tax, the market price of investment goods is below the price of consumption goods so as to provide the incentive for investment.

[j] Under the three VATs and the personal consumption tax, the sale of investment goods incurs a tax.

[k] Under the sales tax, the price of investment goods is already less than the price of consumption goods; thus, all consumption taxes drive the value of investment goods to $-t$.

[l] Under the income tax, with depreciation allowances that track market value, existing investment goods sell at par with new ones.

[m] Given the assumption that the sale of an existing house has no tax consequences for any of the six taxes, the prices of new and existing houses will be on par. I have assumed that all the consumption taxes treat new houses as consumption goods, so the prices of new houses are on par with consumption.

thing called competitiveness. This idea receives no support from economics. Real exchange rates will change to offset the tax change. Whether this occurs as a change in the nominal rate as well depends on the behavior of the price level, a topic deferred to Section 5.

Third, all the consumption taxes depress the price of existing capital goods. Whereas, under an income tax, the owner of capital goods can convert them to consumption without paying additional taxes, the same conversion incurs the consumption tax in all cases. Under the VATs, the tax is paid directly by the business if sales of existing capital are counted as negative investment. If not, the same effect occurs because used capital will not qualify for the tax deduction given to newly produced capital. Under the sales tax, both the prices of new and existing capital are depressed by the amount of the tax, and under a personal consumption tax, the sale of capital goods is taxed as negative saving. The depression of the price of existing capital is a more precise statement of a point made frequently in different language: the move from income to consumption taxation imposes double taxes on existing saving. It was taxed first under the income tax and now will be taxed again under the consumption tax. The statement is clearly true for direct ownership of capital goods. Its truth for savings in nominal financial claims depends on the price level issues to be considered in Section 5.

Finally, Table 1 reveals no transition issues for housing. Both the income tax and the consumption tax in all its variants leave the price of houses on par with goods consumption. This conclusion is overreaching for two reasons: (1) it considers housing to be a completely produced good and does not consider the price of land, and (2) it looks at housing only from the supply side; in the short run, the demand for housing will affect the prices of existing houses. I take up the housing demand issues in Section 7.

Stock Prices

As a simplification, think of equity as direct ownership of capital goods. The consumption tax depresses the purchasing power of the existing capital stock. Domestic equity holders suffer capital losses from consumption tax reform. The destination VAT and the sales tax keep foreign equity holders whole because these taxes lower the price of traded goods in terms of domestic consumption goods by the same amount.[1] The

---

[1] This point may be easier to see if one supposes that the price of domestic consumption goods rises by the amount of the tax. Neither the price of equity nor the price of traded goods changes at all. Domestic shareholders suffer a loss of purchasing power, but foreign equity holders can still buy the same volume of goods with their shares as they could before tax reform.

origin VAT and Hall–Rabushka impose the same loss on foreign equity holders as on domestic ones.

5. NOMINAL PRICES AND PRICE MEASUREMENT

Prediction of the effects on nominal prices as the result of the transition to a consumption tax enters the tricky territory of price-level economics. Under monetary neutrality, the price level is chosen unilaterally by the central bank. An event such as tax reform affects the price level only to the extent that it makes the central bank choose a different target.

With monetary nonneutrality, there is more to say, although of course the central bank unambiguously chooses the price level in the longer run. The biggest issue is how nominal prices and wages achieve the decline in the real product wage required under a VAT or sales tax. Either the price level must rise or the wage level must fall. If the latter is ruled out as impractical, then the economy needs a quick burst of inflation. If the inflation triggers indexation, there may be further problems. British adoption of the VAT in 1979 put the economy through this type of cycle.

The central problem is the wage contract. Under the income tax, wages are set on a pretax basis. Workers pay taxes from their earnings. The taxes that put wages on an after-tax basis—the VATs and the sales tax—call for either a price change or a wage change to accommodate the switch. One way is for wages to fall by the amount of the tax. Except for effects caused by changes in tax rates, there would then be no change in after-tax wages, and prices would not have to change. Evidence on the nature of the wage contract suggests that it would be difficult to bring about the immediate wage cut. The other way to accommodate the change is for prices to rise. Then the wage contract is honored in nominal terms, but real after-tax earnings are kept stable in the face of tax reform by the price increase. For a price increase to work, it is essential that there be no feedback from prices to wages. In an economy with full cost-of-living escalation of wages, no price increase would be large enough to get the real after-tax wage back down to its appropriate level.

The best answer would appear to be to encourage firms to reset prices on the day that the tax becomes effective by the amount of the tax and then to define the cost-of-living index to exclude the VAT or sales tax. The goal is to get the price level to rise immediately but not to develop any momentum, and to prevent wages from changing at all.

The taxes that leave wages on a pretax basis—Hall–Rabushka and the personal consumption tax—do not encounter this problem at all. The existing wage and price levels remain the appropriate levels after tax reform.

The assumption in the remainder of the present paper is that the standard VATs (but not Hall–Rabushka) and the sales tax cause a one-time increase in the prices of consumption goods, and the other taxes leave the price level unchanged. This assumption is stated in the first line of Table 2.

5.1 Nominal Exchange Rates

As noted in Section 4, the destination VAT and the sales tax drive wedges between domestic consumption goods prices and the prices of traded goods. As a result, they affect real exchange rates in the same way. If, as previously suggested, the right accommodation to a VAT or sales tax is an immediate jump in the nominal price level, then nominal exchange rates need not change. However, it will not be possible to introduce a VAT as a complete surprise and raise the price level by 20 percent in the same millisecond. The foreign exchange market will be perturbed by expectations.

These conclusions are summarized in the second and third lines of Table 2.

5.2 Value of Debt Claims

With respect to debt, the issue is the change in the price level. It is both realistic and desirable for the domestic price of consumption goods to rise by the amount of a VAT or sales tax. Thus, debt holders suffer a loss of purchasing power over domestic consumption goods equal to the amount of the tax, for these taxes. Foreign debt holders come out even in relation to traded goods for the destination-basis VAT and the sales tax and lose under the origin-basis VAT. No changes in any of these nominal variables or in the purchasing power of debt would need to occur under Hall–Rabushka or a personal consumption tax.

The conclusions about the purchasing power of debt are summarized in the fourth and fifth lines of Table 2. They shed some more light on the issue of the double taxation of existing saving as a result of a move from income to consumption taxation. Under the standard VATs and the sales tax, where a one-time rise in the price level is needed to accommodate the tax, the loss in purchasing power of nominal debt creates double taxation. Under the personal consumption tax, there is no change in the purchasing power of debt, but the act of consuming will be taxed, so again there is double taxation. Only under Hall–Rabushka, of the five consumption taxes, is there no double taxation of existing saving in the form of debt.

TABLE 2
Effects on Nominal Measures

	Destination-basis VAT	Origin-basis VAT	Consumption sales tax	Hall–Rabushka	Personal consumption tax
Nominal price of consumption goods	↑	↑	↑	0	0
Nominal price of traded goods	0	↑	0	0	0
Nominal exchange rate	0	↓	0	0	0
Value of dollar debt in relation to consumption goods	↓	↓	↓	0	0
Value of dollar debt in relation to traded goods	0	↓	0	0	0

↑, rise by amount of tax; ↓, fall by amount of tax; 0, no change.

6. INTEREST RATES AND RELATED ISSUES

The most complicated and interesting issues about the move to consumption taxation involve interest rates and asset markets. The discussion of these issues is necessarily tentative because there are large unresolved questions in the economics of consumption that bear directly on the issues.

6.1 Fundamental Analysis

Although the fundamental analysis, based on the life-cycle theory of consumption, does not seem to answer many of the questions about the operation of world capital markets, it provides a good point of departure. In an economy where people live for many decades, or where families have common budget constraints from one generation to the next, the growth of consumption is governed by the Euler equation,

$$\dot{c}/c = \sigma[(1 - \tau)r - \rho], \qquad (1)$$

where c is consumption; σ is the intertemporal elasticity of substitution in consumption; τ is the income tax rate on interest; and ρ is the rate of impatience. See Hall (1988) for a discussion of the rationalization of equation (1).

Under the further assumption that in the steady state, the growth of consumption is the exogenous growth rate g, of the whole economy, I conclude that

$$r = \frac{\rho + g/\sigma}{1 - \tau}. \qquad (2)$$

A consumption tax changes the income tax rate τ to zero. If the rate were previously, say, 30 percent, the interest rate should decline by 43 percent on a switch to consumption taxation. Many important conclusions about the transition would follow if this drop occurred quickly.

The discussion of the reasons that interest rates do not drop sharply and immediately can be divided into three parts:

1. the decline cannot take effect until there has been enough extra investment to drive down the marginal product of capital;
2. large amounts of interest income are not currently taxed; and
3. the United States is embedded in a world capital market.

6.2 Timing of Interest Decline in a Theoretical Model of a Closed Economy

The effect of tax reform is well understood in a closed competitive economy with a single type of output, a single type of capital, and life-cycle consumers (Hall, 1971). Assume for simplicity that the imposition of the consumption tax is a surprise, so that there is no intertemporal substitution effect from the consumption tax. The market interest rate in the economy is the net marginal product of capital. Assume, for the moment, that labor supply is inelastic. Because the tax reform does not affect the capital stock and because there is no change in the level of employment, the interest rate does not change initially. However, the consumption Euler equation shifts because the income tax rate τ has fallen to zero. Consumption must grow faster; that is, consumers must defer consumption to take advantage of the higher incentive to save. Consequently, consumption falls discontinuously at the time of tax reform. The extra output is invested. As the capital stock rises, the interest rate falls. As the interest rate approaches its new lower level, consumption growth declines to equal the rate of growth of output.

At reasonable parameter values, the convergence to the new steady state with more capital and a lower interest rate is largely completed within a decade. If labor supply is elastic and is governed by life-cycle principles, then the convergence is faster. The immediate effect of tax reform is to stimulate labor supply, which elevates the interest rate in the short run. The immediate depression of consumption is greater and the rate of capital accumulation more rapid.

6.3 The Extent of Income Taxation of Interest Income

The model just discussed is a great oversimplification of the U.S. tax system. Large amounts of business income are paid out as interest but not taxed under the personal income tax (Gordon and Slemrod, 1988). In fact, only a tiny fraction of all interest paid is reported as income under the personal tax. The tax treatment of saving for retirement operates on the consumption principle, in particular.

6.4 Interaction of the U.S. Economy and the Rest of the World

The U.S. capital markets are tightly integrated with those of other major industrial countries, notably Japan, Britain, and Germany. Those countries rely on a mixture of consumption and income taxation and presumably would not change their tax systems on U.S. tax reform. The analysis of tax reform in the open U.S. economy has to consider the general equilibrium in a world economy with heterogeneous tax systems.

The general equilibrium analysis encounters a basic problem, as a number of earlier authors have observed. Equation (2), describing the interest rate in the long run, ought to apply to each country, with parameters specific to the country. But a world capital market should have a single real interest rate. The biggest paradox is for growth rates. High-growth countries like Japan should have chronically higher interest rates, according to the life-cycle theory. In fact, real interest rates seem to be roughly equal among the major countries with open capital markets. Although expected changes in real exchange rates can support differences in real interest rates in the short run, neither theory nor actual experience suggests that this mechanism works in the long run.

Tax reform in the United States would encounter the same paradox. How can the U.S. interest rate fall if interest rates in Japan and elsewhere remain locked in place by equation (2)? The answer to both the growth and tax paradoxes appears to be that real interest rates for equivalent traded securities are equalized in world markets, but households see rewards for saving that are sufficiently different to satisfy equation (2) separately for each country's parameters.

Differences in internal capital markets among countries may be an important part of the resolution of the paradox. For example, direct controls on borrowing may prevent Japanese households from having the high levels of debt that would be needed to satisfy the life-cycle model's prescription for scheduling consumption in a high-growth, low-interest economy. On the other hand, the U.S. consumer is in fairly direct contact with world capital markets. Interest rates in the most important credit market for households, the mortgage market, are tightly linked to world rates.

In world equilibrium, firms and intermediaries in countries with naturally high interest rates (with high growth rates and high income tax rates) will be net suppliers of bonds in world markets. Equilibrium occurs where the marginal cost of issuing more bonds is equated, after risk adjustment, to the costs of other sources of funds and to the marginal benefit from investing the funds. Patterns of specialization in the issuance of securities should track differences in fundamental interest rates, as described by equation (2).

In the resulting equilibrium, there may be scope for a considerable effect of tax reform on U.S. interest rates. First, the United States is about one third of the total world capital market. Second, relatively modest changes in the pattern of specialization in world securities markets may be enough to reach the new equilibrium in which the world interest rates have moved most of the way to the point predicted by equation (2) for the United States.

7. HOUSING

The fear that consumption taxation would wipe out housing values is one of the major political obstacles to tax reform. The factors entering the analysis of this sensitive issue are the following:

1. A consumption tax stimulates demand for investment goods, such as houses.
2. All the consumption taxes considered here place a new tax on the rental value of the structural part of owner-occupied housing, which will reduce the demand for housing.
3. The price of land in the long run and structures in the short run will fall as a result of the elimination of the personal tax deduction for mortgage interest.
4. The price of land will rise as the interest rate falls.

7.1 Houses as Investment Goods

It will be useful to imagine that houses are treated as investment goods under a new consumption tax. That is, the effective price of a new house is lower than the effective price of consumption by the amount of the consumption tax. For example, under a sales tax, new houses would be exempt from tax. By itself, this element of the consumption tax would stimulate housing demand, just as a consumption tax will stimulate demand for plants and equipment.

7.2 Taxation of the Rental Value of Owner-Occupied Structures

All the taxes considered here impose the consumption tax on the service value of housing structures. The failure of the existing income tax to tax the service value of consumer durables, including housing, has been the subject of extensive commentary. The case for federal taxation of housing services is uneasy, however, because state and local property taxes already put the equivalent of a tax on housing services. The addition of a federal tax might push the balance too far in the direction of a bias against housing. A further complication is that some of the state and local taxes finance personal consumption and should not be considered taxes at all.

None of the consumption taxes actually measures and taxes the value of the services of houses. Instead, they impose an equivalent tax at the time that houses are built. Contractors would pay the VATs, the sales tax, or the Hall–Rabushka tax, and there would be no provision for families to deduct the cost of a new house. Structures would be on an equal footing whether they were owned or rented. In the rental situation, the landlord would receive an immediate write-off for the new structure and would then pay tax on the rental receipts. The two should be equal in present value. Eliminating both sides, as in the case of owner occupancy, leaves the substance of the tax unaffected.

Note that the treatment of houses as investment goods calls for removing the taxation of new house production, whereas the taxation of the flow of services calls for replacing exactly the same tax. The combination of treating houses as investments and of bringing their service flows into the tax base is an exact wash. Under all the consumption taxes considered here, housing does not participate in the investment boom that would accompany tax reform because of the extension of taxation to housing services.

7.3 Elimination of the Mortgage Deduction

As a general matter, the deductibility of interest under an income tax is purely an administrative question and has no economic substance. If all taxpayers were subject to interest taxation in the first place, the removal of all interest deductions and the companion removal of all interest taxation would simply result in interest rates that were lower by the amount of the income tax. In this world, removing the mortgage deduction would have almost no effect, even in the short run, on housing.

The U.S. income tax is far from the simple entity just described. Many interest recipients are not taxed, and the personal tax permits deduction only of interest on borrowing against securities and houses. To some extent, the demand for houses is increased and the demand for cars is decreased because houses permit deductible borrowing and cars do not. Interestingly, although the personal tax treatment of interest on borrowing against securities is identical to that for houses, nobody has characterized the deduction of interest on securities as a "subsidy" to securities.

Under the modern U.S. income tax, only higher income taxpayers take itemized deductions. The impact of the elimination of the benefit associated with deductibility of interest on mortgages would necessarily be limited to the upper end of the housing market.

I conclude that removal of the tax deduction for mortgage interest would be a small negative influence in the short run for the price of housing structures and in the short and long run for land prices.

7.4 Lower Interest Rates

The switch to consumption taxation will cause lower interest rates in the longer run. Recall that land is not brought under consumption taxation under any of the proposals. The price of land would rise immediately as a result of the anticipation of lower future interest rates.

7.5 Conclusions on Housing

On net, I believe that the consumption tax reforms considered in the present paper would have a modest negative effect on housing prices and demand. If the reforms did not extend taxation to housing services, there would be a substantial stimulus to housing demand. The effect on housing prices would depend on how the consumption taxes avoided the taxation of services.

Under a sales tax, an easy way to avoid taxing housing services would be to exempt new houses from the tax. Houses would then fail to participate in the jump in prices that would affect consumption goods. Under all the other taxes, the purchaser would need to be given a deduction or rebate at the time of purchase. For the standard VATs and Hall–Rabushka, it is hard to see how this could be done in practice. For the VATs, some type of personal tax return just for this purpose would have to be created. For Hall–Rabushka, the loss carryforward mechanism currently present in the business tax return would have to appear on the personal return. For a personal consumption tax based on the cash-flow principle, the deduction would be straightforward, but only because that tax is so complicated to begin with.

The ease of accommodating a more generous treatment of housing may tilt the balance of tax reform toward a national sales tax. Alternatively, under Hall–Rabushka or any consumption tax system that has a personal return, it would be attractive to create a deduction related to home ownership. For example, homeowners could deduct double their state and local property taxes. The effect would be to lower the rate of federal taxation of housing services to reflect the high existing rates under state and local property taxes.

The inclusion of a deduction based on property taxes could more than offset the adverse effects of tax reform on housing.

8. HUMAN CAPITAL

Most human capital formation is already taxed on the consumption basis and would remain so under tax reform. When a student foregoes earnings in order to go to school, or a worker earns a lower cash wage because of the value of training on the job, the investment is receiving immediate write-off under either tax system. The cash expenses incurred by an employer who provides training on the job are generally given immediate write-off as well.

The cash expenses of education or training incurred by individuals are not given consumption-tax treatment today. Under the sales tax, firms and schools could be exempted. Under Hall–Rabushka and the personal consumption tax, individuals could be given deductions for human capital expenses. Under the VATs, it is unclear how to provide individuals with deductions or rebates. A partial answer is to exempt firms and schools from the VAT, but this does not cover the intermediate products purchased by those organizations.

Much of the cash expense of human capital formation is incurred by governments, particularly state and local ones. Improvements in the efficiency of this process could most likely be achieved by limiting the government's roles to financing education rather than trying to produce it. Within a system of government financed and privately produced education, the issue of providing consumption-tax treatment under the federal tax system to education could be resolved along with the more general issue of the role of the federal government in financing education.

9. DOUBLE TAXATION OF EXISTING SAVINGS

A common criticism of consumption tax reform is that savings accumulated from after-tax income under an income tax will be taxed again as it is consumed. The design of a consumption tax may need to include transition provisions to deal with this issue. A companion issue is the treatment of tax-deferred saving in retirement plans.

Section 3 explained that different consumption taxes impose different patterns of double taxation and windfalls. Table 3 summarizes the effects for debt and equity for savings currently held in after-tax and tax-deferred form.

The VATs and the sale tax raise the price level and thereby deny the holders of debt the purchasing power they expected. There is no effect on the purchasing power of debt and no tax consequence from using debt to finance consumption under Hall–Rabushka. Under the personal consumption tax, a tax is imposed on consumption financed from debt.

The second line of Table 3, showing double taxation of equity held in after-tax form under the income tax, reflects the conclusion in the next-to-last line in Table 1 that the value of investment goods to their owners (the shareholders) is depressed by the amount of the tax by all consumption taxes.

For tax-deferred debt, in the case of the VATs and the sales tax, the removal of income taxes at the time of distribution is offset by the increase in the price level, and there is no net effect. For Hall–Rabushka, there is a windfall from the elimination of the expected income tax and no offsetting event. For the personal consumption tax, the new tax takes the place of the expected income tax, and there is no double tax or

TABLE 3
Effects on Existing Saving

	Destination-basis VAT	Origin-basis VAT	Consumption sales tax	Hall–Rabushka	Personal consumption tax
After-tax debt	→	→	→	0	→
After-tax equity	→	→	→	→	0
Tax-deferred debt (retirement)	0	0	0	←	0
Tax-deferred equity (retirement)	0	0	0	0	0

↑, windfall in amount of tax; ↓, double taxation; 0, no change as a result of tax reform.

windfall. For tax-deferred equity, the decline in the purchasing power of equity replaces the expected income tax for all taxes, and there is no double tax or windfall.

REFERENCES

Gordon, Roger H., and Joel Slemrod (1988). "Do We Collect Any Revenue from Taxing Capital Income?" In *Tax Policy and the Economy*, (vol. 2), Lawrence H. Summers, ed. Cambridge, MA: MIT Press.

Hall, Robert E. (1971). "The Dynamic Effects of Fiscal Policy in an Economy with Foresight." *Review of Economic Studies* 38 (April): 229–244.

———. (1988) "Intertemporal Substitution in Consumption." *Journal of Political Economy* 96 (April): 339–357.

———, and Alvin Rabushka (1995). *The Flat Tax*. Stanford: Hoover Institution Press.

THE EFFECT OF INCREASED TAX RATES ON TAXABLE INCOME AND ECONOMIC EFFICIENCY: A PRELIMINARY ANALYSIS OF THE 1993 TAX RATE INCREASES

Martin Feldstein
Harvard University and NBER

Daniel Feenberg
NBER

EXECUTIVE SUMMARY

The 1993 tax legislation raised marginal tax rates from 31 to 36 percent on taxable incomes between $140,000 and $250,000 and to 39.6 percent on incomes above $250,000. This paper uses recently published Internal Revenue Service (IRS) data on taxable incomes by adjusted gross income (AGI)

Martin Feldstein is Professor of Economics at Harvard University and President of the National Bureau of Economic Research. Daniel Feenberg is a Research Associate of the NBER. We are grateful to Larry Lindsey and Larry Summers for discussions about this research and to participants in the National Bureau of Economic Research Conference on Tax Policy and the Economy, Washington, D.C., November 7, 1995, for comments on an earlier draft. This study is part of the NBER Research Program on the Economic Effects of Taxation.

class to analyze how the 1993 tax rate increases affected taxable income, tax revenue, and economic efficiency. Our estimates are based on a difference-in-difference procedure that compares the growth of taxable incomes among taxpayers with AGIs over $200,000 with that of incomes of lower income taxpayers. We use the NBER TAXSIM model to adjust for interyear differences in the composition of the two taxpayer groups.

The results show that high-income taxpayers would have reported 7.8 percent more taxable income in 1993 than they did if their tax rates had not increased. Because of the high threshold for the increase in tax rates, this decline in taxable income caused the Treasury to lose more than half of the extra revenue that would have been collected if taxpayers had not changed their behavior.

The deadweight loss caused by the higher marginal tax rates (including the effects on labor supply and on consumption of goods and services favored by deductions and exclusions) is approximately twice as large as the $8 billion in revenue raised by the 1993 tax rate.

Several possible statistical biases could cause the estimated effect of the tax changes to either underestimate or overestimate the true long-run effect. The paper concludes with a discussion of these problems and of plans for future analysis.

1. INTRODUCTION

Although several studies have shown that lowering income tax rates in the 1980s raised taxable income and labor supply,[1] there are no studies of the effects of increases in marginal tax rates. The present paper fills that gap by analyzing taxpayer behavior after the 1993 increase in personal tax rates using data from 1993 tax returns recently released by the Treasury.[2]

The sensitivity of taxable income to changes in marginal tax rates is obviously important because it determines the effect of tax rate changes on revenue. Less obvious, the deadweight loss that results from a

---

[1] Lindsey (1987), Eissa (1996), and Navratil (1995) studied the effect of the 1981 tax rate reductions on taxable income and on the labor supply of married women. Feenberg and Poterba (1993), Auten and Carroll (1994a), Eissa (1995), Feldstein (1995a,b), and Navratil (1995) studied the effects of the 1986 tax rate reductions. The actual panel data used by Auten and Carroll (1994a) and Feldstein (1995a) show that despite the inherent problems with the synthetic panels used in other studies, the results of those studies are very much in line with the more accurate panel data. See also Auerbach (1994, 1995) for evidence on the tendency of official revenue forecasts to overstate actual revenue because of taxpayer responses.

[2] The earlier draft of this paper that was distributed to conference participants was based on the preliminary IRS tax statistics for 1993 (Cruciano, 1995), whereas the current version uses the final IRS statistics for 1993.

change in marginal tax rates is proportional to the compensated elasticity of taxable income with respect to the net of tax rate.[3] For both reasons, it is important to estimate the effect of tax rate changes on taxable income.

In this paper, we report the results of a preliminary analysis of the effects of the 1993 tax rate increases. The analysis is consistent with the basic finding of the previous studies of the tax rate decreases of the 1980s that taxable income is quite sensitive to marginal tax rates. Our estimates imply that the rise in marginal tax rates in 1993 led to a substantial decline in taxable income. As a result of this sensitivity, the 1993 tax rate increases raised less than one half of the revenue that would have been raised with no behavioral response.[4,5]

Moreover, the compensated elasticity of taxable income with respect to the net of tax rate (i.e., 1 minus the marginal tax rate) that we estimate on the basis of the 1993 behavior implies that the deadweight loss associated with the 1993 tax rate increases is nearly twice as large as the net revenue raised by those rate increases. This means that for every dollar of additional revenue collected by the government as a result of the higher tax rates, taxpayers experience a decline in their well-being equivalent to $3 as a result of the induced changes in work, in the form of compensation, and in tax deductible expenditures.

Section 2 of this paper reviews the nature of the 1993 tax increases and the ways in which the resulting income and substitution effects could affect representative taxpayers. Section 3 discusses the data and method

---

[3] See Feldstein (1995c) for a demonstration that the overall deadweight loss of the income tax that results from distortions in labor supply, in tax deductible expenditures, and in the form of compensation is proportional to the elasticity of taxable income with respect to the net of tax rate (i.e., 1 minus the marginal tax rate).

[4] Feldstein and Feenberg (1993) analyzed the proposed 1993 tax rate increases and estimated that taxpayer responses might cut the projected revenue by about 50 percent if taxpayers responded to the higher marginal tax rates by reducing their taxable incomes by 5 percent. That analysis used TAXSIM data on individual tax returns (for 1989 adjusted to 1993 levels) but did not have actual taxpayer experience on which to base the estimated response of taxable income. Feldstein (1995a) showed that an elasticity of one of taxable income with respect to the net of tax rate would eliminate virtually all of the projected tax revenue.

[5] In the language of Washington tax policy analysis, the actual revenue effect of the tax rate increases was less than one half of the "static" forecast. The U.S. Treasury Department's revenue estimate was not strictly a static forecast but assumed that behavioral changes would reduce 1993 personal income tax revenue by 7 percent as taxpayers responded to the higher marginal tax rates by changes in realized capital gains, in the use of tax-exempt bonds, in shifts from subchapter S to subchapter C corporations, and in various forms of noncompliance and tax sheltering (Auten and Carroll, 1994). The method used by the Treasury and the Joint Committee on Taxation of the Congress explicitly ignores changes in labor supply, in the form of compensation, and in a variety of deductions (Auten and Carroll, 1994; Feldstein, 1994).

used in the current analysis. Section 4 describes our estimated taxpayer responses and the implied net revenue effects of the 1993 tax rate increases. In Section 5 we present the implied elasticities. Section 6 reports the associated deadweight losses of the tax rate increases. Section 7 applies the estimated elasticities to calculate the effect of eliminating the ceiling on the health insurance payroll tax base that began in January 1994. Section 8 discusses possible biases in our estimate of taxpayer responses, including the relation between the observed short-term effects and the likely longer term effects. Finally, Section 9 summarizes conclusions and caveats and points to the direction for future research.

2. THE 1993 TAX RATE INCREASES

The tax legislation enacted in 1993 raised the marginal tax rate from 31 to 36 percent on taxable incomes between $140,000 and $250,000 (between $115,000 and $250,000 for single taxpayers) and to 39.6 percent on taxable income in excess of $250,000.[6] In addition, the legislation eliminated the $135,000 ceiling on the Medicare component of the payroll tax, effectively adding an additional 2.9 percent combined employer–employee tax on the compensation component of taxable income. Because this Hospital Insurance (HI) payroll tax did not come into effect until January 1994, we ignore it in our calculations. To the extent that high-income taxpayers recognized that their marginal tax rates would rise in 1994 and responded by shifting compensation to 1993, the observed reduction in taxable income in 1993 is smaller than it would otherwise be, and we underestimate the longer run loss of tax revenue and the implied sensitivity of taxes to the net of tax rate. We can, however, use our estimates of the sensitivity of taxable income to tax rates to estimate the effect of the higher HI tax base. We return to do this in Section 5.[7]

Because the marginal tax rate applies only to incomes over a very high threshold, for most of the high-income taxpayers there is a substantial increase in the marginal tax rate but little increase in the average tax rate

---

[6] Because of the loss of 3 percent of itemized deductions at high-income levels, the effective marginal tax rates are about 1 percent higher than the statutory 31, 36, and 39.6 percent rates that we use in our calculations. We ignore this in our calculations.

[7] The 1993 legislation also increased the tax rate for the alternative minimum tax (AMT) and changed the AMT rules to broaden its base. Since the AMT only collects an incremental $1.1 billion, or 0.8 percent of tax revenue, among the high-income taxpayers whom we study, we ignore it in our analysis. To the extent that some taxpayers became subject to the AMT as a result of the 1993 legislation, they would have experienced a decline in their marginal tax rate and may have responded by increasing their taxable income. Since we do not take the AMT into account explicitly in our analysis, such behavior would cause us to underestimate the effect of higher marginal tax rates on taxpayer behavior.

on their initial ("no behavioral response") income. The structure of the tax rate increase therefore has the likely effect of reducing taxable income for many taxpayers to such an extent that the revenue with the higher marginal tax rates is very much smaller than the traditional "static" (no behavioral response) estimates would imply.[8]

An analysis of two representative high-income taxpayers shows how this would occur in practice. Consider first a couple with $180,000 of taxable income, the level of income that the Clinton administration identified as the median income among those taxpayers whose tax rates were increased in the 1993 legislation. With no behavioral response, the increase in the marginal tax rate from 0.31 to 0.36 on taxable income between $140,000 and $180,000 would raise additional revenue of $2,000. However, the tax rate increase reduces the net of tax share that the taxpayer receives from 0.69 to 0.64, a decrease of 7.2 percent. If this decrease in the net of tax share causes taxable income to decline by 5 percent,[9] taxable income falls from $180,000 to $171,000. This reduces the personal income tax revenue by 31 percent of the $9,000 decline in taxable income, a revenue decrease of $2,790. The combination of this revenue loss and of the additional $1,550 collected by levying a 5 percent tax on the $31,000 of taxable income (the difference between $171,000 of taxable income and the threshold of $140,000 for the higher tax rate) causes the income tax liability of this couple to decline by $1,240 as a result of the tax change.

There may also be a loss of Old Age, Survivor, and Disability Insurance (OASDI) and Hospital Insurance (HI) payroll tax revenue. For example, if the $180,000 of taxable income reflected the husband's wage income of $130,000 and the wife's wage of $50,000 (plus investment income equal to itemized deductions and other adjustments), the decline in taxable income could reduce the HI tax revenue at a 2.9 percent rate if part of the decline is due to a reduction in the husband's taxable compensation and could reduce the OASDI and HI revenue at a 15.3 percent rate if part of the decline in taxable income is due to a reduction in the wife's compensation. Our analysis assumes that the compensation of the husband and the compensation of the wife both decline in the same proportion as overall taxable income.[10] Reducing the husband's wage income by 5 percent of

---

[8] We emphasized this in Feldstein and Feenberg (1993) and Feldstein (1995a).

[9] A 5 percent decline of taxable income in response to the 7.2 percent decline in the net of tax share is roughly in line with the evidence presented in this paper and less than the decline implied by the evidence presented by Auten and Carroll (1994a), Lindsey (1987), and Feldstein (1995a).

[10] See Feldstein and Feenberg (1995) for our method of distributing total wage and salary income between husbands and wives. We also include adding 50 percent of business and professional income (schedule C income) to the husband's taxable compensation.

$130,000 implies a loss of HI tax revenue of $188. Reducing the wife's wage income by 5 percent of $50,000 implies a loss of OASDI and HI tax revenue of $382. The total revenue loss caused by the higher personal tax rate is thus the sum of the lost personal tax revenue ($1,240) and the loss of the payroll tax revenue ($570), for a total revenue loss of $1,810.

The revenue effect of the increase in 1993 tax rates becomes positive at higher levels of taxable income. Consider the effect on a couple with taxable income of $500,000, including $300,000 of taxable compensation of the husband and $50,000 of taxable compensation of the wife. Their marginal tax rate rises from 0.31 to 0.396, reducing the net of tax share from 0.69 to 0.604, a decline of 12.7 percent. Assume that this induces a decline in taxable income of 8 percent, from $500,000 to $460,000.[11] The net effect on personal income tax revenue is therefore an additional 5 percent tax on the income between $140,000 and $250,000 (a tax increase of $5,500), an additional 8.6 percent on the income between $250,000 and $460,000 (a tax increase of $18,060), and a loss of revenue at the initial 31 percent on the reduced $40,000 (a tax decrease of $12,400); the net effect is therefore a net personal income tax rise of $11,160. The offsetting loss of payroll tax revenue is small, since the decline in the husband's wage and salary income is all in the untaxed range above $135,000. The 8 percent decline in the wife's wage income from $50,000 causes a $612 loss of payroll tax revenue, bringing the government's overall net revenue gain to $10,518. For comparison, the static revenue estimate based on the assumption that taxable income would remain at $500,000 would be $27,000. The actual revenue gain for this couple is thus only slightly more than one third of the static estimate.

We had planned to study the actual effects of the 1993 tax changes as soon as the Treasury Department's panel data for 1993 became available, using the method applied to the 1986 data in Feldstein (1995a). We were struck, however, by an article in the *New York Times* that appeared on April 17, 1995 with the headline "Well-to-Do Paid 16% More in Taxes in '93, Study Says."

The story reported that "The taxes of well-to-do Americans surged 16 percent in 1993, the first year of revisions pressed into law by President Clinton. People who earned $100,000 or more owed the Government $31 billion more, compared with their tax bills in 1992 according to computer assisted analysis of IRS data by the Associated Press. Everyone else owed about $3 billion more."

It was not clear to us why the analysis included the more than 3 million taxpayers with incomes between $100,000 and $200,000 of AGIs,

---

[11] See footnote 9 about the plausibility of this magnitude of response.

since few of them would have been affected by the increase in marginal tax rates on taxable incomes over $140,000. In contrast, the average taxable income among taxpayers with AGIs of $200,000 is slightly more than $140,000. Among the fewer than 1 million taxpayers with AGIs over $200,000, 98 percent were affected by the increase in tax rates, whereas only 9.5 percent of taxpayers with AGIs between $100,000 and $200,000 were affected. We suspected, moreover, that the general rise in the taxes paid by households with incomes over $100,000 reflected the rise in nominal incomes and the shift of taxpayers who were not affected by the 1993 tax rate increases into higher tax brackets.

The study reported in the *New York Times* was widely noted as evidence that the 1993 tax rates had raised substantial revenue at the top and that the direct revenue effect of higher marginal tax rates had not been offset by reductions in taxable income. Since the individual taxpayer panel data would not be available for several years, we decided to investigate the available aggregate evidence in more detail.

3. THE DATA AND METHOD OF ANALYSIS

Our analysis uses the Treasury Department's recently published tabulations based on the individual income tax returns for 1993. These tabulations provide information on taxable income and other tax return items classified by AGI class. We focus our analysis on taxpayers with an AGI greater than $200,000 and ask how this group, which we refer to as *high-income taxpayers,* responded to the 1993 tax changes.

Since we do not have data for the same individual taxpayers in 1992 and 1993, we cannot examine how the actual taxable incomes of the 1992 high-income taxpayers changed between those two years. We can, however, estimate how adjusted taxable income changed for the highest income taxpayers as a group between 1992 and 1993.[12] We compare the observed change in the taxable incomes of these high-income taxpayers with our estimate of what that change would have been if they had not modified their taxable income in response to the rise in tax rates.

We base this estimate of their no-behavioral-response 1993 taxable incomes on the behavior of taxpayers with AGIs between $50,000 and $200,000.[13] In effect, we assume that the relative distribution of income would have remained the same (with all taxpayers subject to a common

---

[12] This is essentially the method used by Lindsey (1987).

[13] About 93 percent of high-income taxpayers were subject to marginal tax rates of 36 or 39.6 percent; in contrast, only 2 percent of taxpayers with AGIs of $50,000 to $200,000 were taxed at these high rates. These figures are based on our analysis of the Treasury Department's 1991 Public Use Sample of tax returns adjusted to 1993 levels.

percent rise) and attribute the difference from this benchmark to the tax change.[14]

Because the tax rate increases did not apply to capital gains (recall that the tax on capital gains remained at a maximum of 28 percent), we look at taxable income excluding capital gains taxed at 28 percent. We also adjust the measure of taxable income by adding back in the personal exemptions and standard deductions because their values changed between 1992 and 1993.[15] We call the resulting figure *adjusted taxable income* (ATI).

Our estimate of what ATIs would have been in 1993 among high-income taxpayers if there had been no change in behavior is derived with the help of the NBER TAXSIM model, using individual tax returns for 1991, the most recent year for which such data are available. These data are a stratified random sample of more than 100,000 tax returns selected by the IRS to overweight high-income returns. We begin by "aging" these data to 1992 in a way that causes the ATI among 1992 high-income taxpayers to match the published amount.[16] This sample of synthetic 1992 individual tax returns is then used to derive a baseline sample of 1993 high-income tax returns corresponding to the 1992 tax rules (or, equivalently, to the assumption that adoption of the 1993 tax rules did not change taxpayer behavior).

The key to deriving this synthetic sample of no-behavioral-response 1993 high-income tax returns is to assume that the taxable incomes of the high-income taxpayers would increase at the same rate as the taxable incomes of those with AGIs between $50,000 and $200,000, since their tax rates did not change in 1993.[17] The published statistics for 1993 indi-

---

[14] If anything, the tendency for higher incomes to grow more rapidly than lower incomes (see, e.g., the trend in the data presented in Feenberg and Poterba, 1993) suggests that our method underestimates the no-behavioral-response level of 1993 incomes of high-income taxpayers and therefore underestimates the depressing effect of high marginal tax rates.

Other factors may have influenced the groups' incomes in different ways. This could cause our estimate to overstate or understate the true elasticity. We return to these possible sources of bias later in Section 7.

[15] The personal exemptions and standard deduction are extremely small as a proportion of income for the high-income group. The standard deduction was only $300 million for this group in 1993, less than one tenth of 1 percent of taxable income. Personal exemptions were about one billion or less than one half of 1 percent of taxable income.

[16] In the earlier draft of this paper, prepared for the *Tax Policy and the Economy* Conference, we used the "preliminary" totals for 1993. In the current paper, we are able to use the published "final" totals.

[17] To the extent that some of those in the $50,000 to $200,000 AGI class did experience tax rate increases that reduced their 1993 taxable incomes below what they would otherwise have been, our method of comparing the changes in taxable incomes in the two groups underestimates the effect of the tax rate rise on taxable income. But as noted earlier, on the basis of the 1991 data, we estimate that only 2 percent of taxpayers in the $50,000 to $200,000 AGI class in 1993 would have been subject to higher marginal tax rates.

We also developed an estimate of the baseline no-behavioral-response taxable incomes of

cate that the ATIs of taxpayers with 1993 AGIs of $50,000 to $200,000 was 8.2 percent greater than that of taxpayers with 1992 AGIs of $50,000 to $200,000. This of course does not imply that on average each individual's taxable income rose by 8.2 percent, since the general rise in incomes shifted more taxpayers into the $50,000 to $200,000 AGI class. The TAXSIM data on individual tax returns imply that this 8.2 percent increase in the total income of the $50,000 to $200,000 AGI class occurs if all individual taxable incomes grow by 3.4 percent between 1992 and 1993.[18] This substantial difference shows the danger of trying to base comparisons across years or across income groups on published data by AGI class without using microeconomic data to adjust for the changing composition of the groups.

Having derived this key 3.4 percent individual income growth parameter, we raise the 1992 ATI of every taxpayer by this amount. With this growth of ATI at the individual level, the aggregate ATI among taxpayers with 1993 AGIs over $200,000 would have been $399 billion, an increase of 7.0 percent from the $374 billion in the same AGI class in 1992.

In contrast, the published estimate of ATI among taxpayers with AGIs over $200,000 in 1993 actually declined from $374 billion in 1992 to $364 billion in 1993.[19,20] If the study referred to in the *New York Times* story had divided taxpayers at $200,000 of AGIs (to focus on those who were likely to have experienced high rates), the analysis would have concluded that those with incomes over $200,000 experienced an aggregate decrease of taxable incomes of $3 billion, whereas the taxable incomes of those in lower AGI groups saw their incomes rise by $60 billion.[21]

Part of the observed decline was due to the fact that some taxpayers who had taxable incomes over $200,000 in 1992 dropped into the next

---

the 1993 high-income taxpayers by assuming that their taxable incomes would rise at the same rate as all taxpayers with AGIs below $200,000. Although this procedure is inferior in principle to using the taxpayer with AGIs between $50,000 and $200,000 because the lower income groups are potentially subject to quite different market forces and income composition than the group of taxpayers with incomes between $50,000 and $200,000, the results for this "full-sample group" are very similar to the results for the $50,000 to $200,000 group.

[18] We also rescale the sampling weights to reflect a 1.1 percent increase in the adult population between 1992 and 1993.

[19] Such a reduction is very unusual. In the preceding decade, taxable income excluding capital gains among taxpayers with AGI over $200,000 declined only in 1988 and 1991. The 1991 decline may reflect the increase in the top tax rate that year.

[20] The 1993 adjusted taxable income among taxpayers with AGIs over $200,000 is derived from the total taxable income of $427 billion in this group by subtracting $64 billion of capital gains and adding back in $0.3 billion of standard deductions and $1.5 billion of personal exemptions.

[21] Recall that by looking at AGIs over $100,000, they were able to write that the taxes paid by high-income taxpayers rose $16 billion, whereas the taxable incomes of all others rose only $3 billion. The $3 billion increase refers to full taxable incomes, not just the ATI.

lower AGI class in 1993 as part of their reaction to the higher marginal tax rates. It would of course be inappropriate to compare the no-behavioral-response incomes of those who are projected to have 1993 income over $200,000 to the actual incomes of those with more than $200,000 of AGI without taking into account the taxpayers who migrated to the lower AGI class.

To adjust for this shift in taxpayers, we note that, with the no-behavioral-response assumption, the number of taxpayers with an AGI greater than $200,000 is projected to increase by 80,000 between 1992 and 1993. In contrast, the observed number of taxpayers with AGIs over $200,000 actually increased by only 38,000. We infer that 42,000 taxpayers dropped from the AGI greater than $200,000 class to the lower class. We therefore augment the estimated ATI in the AGI greater than $200,000 class by an estimate of the taxable income of these 42,000 returns. To be conservative, we attribute to these 42,000 taxpayers an average "actual" adjusted taxable income equal to the projected average ATI among 1993 taxpayers with projected no-behavioral-response AGIs between $200,000 and $220,000. This average is $157,000 per return, or a total of $6.6 billion. We add this to the $364 billion of ATI among taxpayers with observed AGIs over $200,000 in 1993 to have a figure of $370 billion of ATI that can be compared with our no-behavioral-response estimate of $399 billion.

4. TAXPAYER RESPONSES AND THE NET REVENUE EFFECTS OF THE 1993 TAX RATE INCREASES

The analysis of Section 3 provides the key estimates that we need to evaluate the effect of the taxpayers' behavior in response to the 1993 tax rate increases. Our analysis implies that if taxpayers had not changed their behavior in response to the higher marginal tax rates, those taxpayers with 1993 AGIs over $200,000 would have reported total ATI (excluding capital gains) of $399 billion, whereas the actual total ATI was $370 billion, a decline of $29 billion, or 7.3 percent.

Consider how this decline in ATI affected tax revenue. Our TAXSIM analysis implies that raising tax rates from 31 to 36 and 39.6 percent would have increased the 1993 tax paid by high-income taxpayers by $19.3 billion if the no-behavioral-response level of ATI ($399 billion) had occurred.[22] In contrast, with the actual modified taxable income reduced

---

[22] This is quite consistent with the original Treasury estimates. Gerald Auten and Robert Carroll of the Treasury's Office of Tax Analysis published the Treasury's estimate of the increase in tax liabilities (Auten and Carroll, 1995). They report a static estimate of $19.5 billion and an estimated net of the long-run behavioral response that is 7 percent less.

to $370 billion, the personal income tax revenue raised with the 1993 tax rates is only $8.8 billion. This implies that taxpayer responses reduced the increase in personal income tax revenue by $10.7 billion. This $10.7 billion revenue leakage due to taxpayer responses was equal to 55 percent of the "static" (no behavioral response) projected revenue gain. In short, the observed experience in 1993 suggests that taxpayer responses reduced the increase in the personal income tax revenue caused by the 1993 tax rate changes to less than one half of what it would have been with no behavioral response.

In addition to this loss of personal tax revenue because of the reduction in taxable incomes, there was also a reduction in high-income and OASDI and HI payroll tax revenues.[23] The $29 billion reduction in taxable income corresponds to a reduction of $1.5 billion of income subject to the full 15.3 percent OASDI and HI rate and to $5.6 billion of compensation subject to the 0.029 percent HI tax. The implied loss of payroll tax revenue is thus $0.38 billion.

Combining the personal tax increases and the losses of OASDI and HI payroll tax revenue implies that the 1993 personal income tax rate changes raised revenue of only $8.4 billion. In comparison to the "static" no-behavioral-response projection of $19.3 billion of additional revenue, this implies a revenue leakage of 57 percent.

5. UNCOMPENSATED AND COMPENSATED ELASTICITIES IMPLIED BY THE 1993 EXPERIENCE

To calculate the compensated elasticity of taxable income with respect to the net of tax rate, we begin with the uncompensated elasticity implied by the evidence in Section 4. We derive this number as the ratio of the percent change in taxable income to the weighted average percent change in the marginal net of tax rates.

The $29 billion reduction in taxable income represents a 7.3 percent decline in taxable income. The percent change in the net of tax rate varies with the type of income and the individual's initial tax level. The lowest percent decreases in the net of tax rate relates to taxpayers with taxable incomes between $140,000 and $250,000 whose compensation exceeded the 1993 threshold for the HI tax of $135,000. For such taxpayers, the marginal tax rate was initially 31 percent, implying a marginal net of tax

---

[23] Recall that the increase in the tax base for the Hospital Insurance payroll tax did not begin until 1994. The calculations reported at this point in the paper therefore refer to the loss of Hospital Insurance and OASDI and Hospital Insurance revenue caused by the reductions in taxable compensation in response to the higher personal income tax rates. The specific effect of the 1994 rise in the Hospital Insurance tax base is discussed later in Section 7.

share of 0.69. The rise in the tax rate to 36 percent implies a percent decline in the net of tax share of 0.05/0.69 = 0.072. The same percent decline applies also to noncompensation income on tax returns with taxable income under $250,000. The largest percent decline in the net of tax share applies to the small amount of wage income that was below the $57,600 ceiling of the OASDI and HI tax base but is on a tax return with total taxable income over $250,000. For such income, the initial marginal tax rate is (0.31 + 0.153)/(1.077) = 0.43 so that the initial net of tax share is 0.57. The increase in the marginal income tax rate to 0.396 implies a decline in the net of tax share to 1 − (0.396 + 0.153)/1.077 = 0.49, a decline of 14 percent. Making a similar calculation for each of the six possible income groups[24] and taking the weighted average (using the amount of income of that type as the weight) produces an average decline in the net of tax share of 11 percent. Thus, the uncompensated elasticity of taxable income with respect to the net of tax share is $\eta = 0.073/0.11 = 0.66$.

This calculation is effectively a difference-in-difference estimator, using the difference between the taxable income changes in 1993 and 1992 for the $50,000–$200,000 AGI class and the $200,000-plus AGI class.

The Compensated Elasticity

The uncompensated elasticity is less than the compensated elasticity that is needed to calculate the deadweight loss of the increased tax rates. The loss of net income caused by the higher tax rates induces taxpayers to work more, make fewer tax-deductible expenditures (e.g., charitable contributions), and take more income in cash rather than untaxed fringe benefits (e.g., attractive offices). This income effect causes the observed uncompensated decline in taxable income to be less than the compensated effect that would occur if there were no loss of net income.

Because the notion of a compensated elasticity of taxable income with respect to the net of tax rate is not a traditional concept,[25] some discussion is warranted. It is useful to begin with the traditional deadweight loss analysis that assumes that taxes distort only the supply of labor. The change in labor supply induced by a change in the net wage can be decomposed into a substitution effect and an income effect:

$$dL/d(1-t)w = \{dL/d(1-t)w\}_{COMP} + (dL/dy)\, dy/d(1-t)w, \qquad (1)$$

[24] For each of the two possible increases in the marginal personal income tax rate (0.05 and 0.086), there are three groups defined by the associated payroll tax rate: wages below $57,600; wages between $57,600 and $135,000; all other wage and nonwage income.

[25] This elasticity is introduced and discussed at length in Feldstein (1995c) on which this portion of the paper draws.

where w is the wage rate; L is leisure (and $1 - L$ is total hours worked); t is the proportional tax rate; and dy is the rise in income that results from the tax rate reduction with no behavioral response. To obtain the corresponding uncompensated and compensated elasticities of labor supply, substitute $1 - L$ for L in each of the three derivatives of equation (1), multiply both sides by $(1 - t)/(1 - L)$. Note that $dy/d(1 - t) = - dy/dt = w(1 - L)$, and write η_L for the uncompensated elasticity on the left-hand side and ϵ_L for the compensated elasticity (the first term on the right-hand side):

$$\eta_L = \epsilon_L + (1 - t)w\, d(1 - L)/dy. \qquad (2)$$

If tax-induced changes in labor supply are the only source of deadweight loss, the increase in the deadweight loss (DWL) caused by an increase in marginal tax rates is given by

$$\Delta\text{DWL} = 0.5\epsilon_L[(t_2^2 - t_1^2)/(1 - t_1)]w(1 - L). \qquad (3)$$

This traditional deadweight loss analysis ignores the effect of changes in the tax rate on the taxpayers' use of deductions and on the shift of compensation to excludable forms (fringe benefits, work environment, etc.). As shown in Feldstein (1995c), the more comprehensive deadweight loss that takes into account deductions and exclusions as well as the labor–leisure substitution can be written in the same form as equation (3) but with the labor supply elasticity replaced by the compensated elasticity of taxable income with respect to the net of tax rate and with labor income $[w(1 - L)]$ replaced by taxable income (TI):

$$\Delta\text{DWL} = 0.5\epsilon_{TI}[(t_2^2 - t_1^2)/(1 - t_1)]\text{TI}. \qquad (4)$$

The compensated elasticity of taxable income can be derived from the uncompensated elasticity that we have estimated here by a decomposition similar to equation (1):

$$d\text{TI}/d(1 - t) = \{d\text{TI}/d(1 - t)\}_{\text{COMP}} + (d\text{TI}/dy)[dy/d(1 - t)], \qquad (5)$$

or, in elasticity form,

$$\eta_{TI} = \epsilon_{TI} + (1 - t)[dt_a/d(1 - t)](d\text{TI}/dy). \qquad (6)$$

where dt_a is the change in the average tax rate (t_a) on taxable income. Since we have an estimate of $\eta_{TI} = 0.66$, we can estimate ϵ_{TI} by calculating the value of $(1-t)[dt_a/d(1-t)](dTI/dy)$. Consider first the value of dTI/dy, the change in ATI that would result from an incremental dollar of exogenous income. An increase in exogenous income induces individuals to increase their consumption of leisure (wL), to spend more on tax deductible items like charitable giving (D), and to take more of their potential compensation in the form of fringe benefits and favorable working conditions, which are excluded from the definition of taxable income (E). Thus, $dTI/dy = -dwL/dy - dD/dy - dE/dy$. The first of these terms is the traditional income effect on the demand for leisure. The labor supply literature suggests that dwL/dy is approximately 0.10 to 0.15.[26]

In an earlier paper, Feldstein (1995c) estimated the effect of an increase in exogenous income on deductible consumption (dD/dy) by a regression analysis of itemized deductions on AGI (using the TAXSIM model with individual tax return data for 1991) holding the marginal rate constant.[27] To focus on those itemized deductions that represent deductible consumption,[28] the measure of deductions used in the regression analyses excludes income taxes paid to state and local governments and nonmortgage interest deductions. Among taxpayers in 1991 in the highest marginal tax bracket (with first dollar marginal tax rates before deductions of 31 percent), the change in deductibles per dollar of AGI was 7.1 cents.

We can think of no good way to estimate the effect of exogenous income on the amount of excluded compensation (dE/dy). A large part of excluded compensation is health benefits, and these are relatively insensitive to income, especially among the very high income taxpayers. Pension funds vary with wages and salaries but are not likely to be affected by the receipt of an exogenous lump-sum income. Other forms of excludable income, including the quality of the work environment, are likely to be more sensitive. We follow Feldstein (1995c) and assign a value of 0.15 to dE/dy.

Combining the three components of $dTI = -dwL/dy - dD/dy - dE/dy$ implies that $dTI/dy = -0.37$. Our data do not allow us to assign different values of dTI/dy to different groups of taxpayers, and any attempt to do so would suggest more information than we have. We therefore use $dTI/dy = -0.37$ for all taxpayers.

[26] The estimated income effect in the labor supply literature is based on the response of participation rates and hours worked. This omits the long-run effect on such things as career choice and location. The restricted definition of labor supply causes the estimated compensated elasticity to be an underestimate of the true long-term response.

[27] This discussion of dTI/dy draws heavily on Feldstein (1995c).

[28] Only those deductions that represent consumption are relevant for calculating the deadweight loss of the distorting effect of tax rates on taxable income (see Feldstein, 1995c).

The other terms in equation (6), $(1 - t)[dt_a/d(1 - t)]$, do differ among taxpayers according to the taxpayer's initial level of taxable income (i.e., the level of income with no behavioral response). The net of tax rate $(1 - t)$ equals 0.69, except on income that is subject at the margin to the social security and Hospital Insurance payroll taxes. Thus, noncompensation income and compensation income above $135,000 have a net of tax rate of 0.69. Compensation that is subject to the 2.9 percent employer–employee rate but not the social security (OASDI and HI) tax (i.e., compensation between $57,600 and $135,000) have an initial marginal tax rate of $(0.31 + 0.029)/(1.0145) = 0.334$, where the denominator of this fraction reflects the employer's share of the payroll tax, implying a net of tax rate of 0.666. Similarly, for those with incomes below $57,600 who were subject to the full 15.3 percent payroll tax, the initial marginal tax rate was $(0.31 + 0.153)/(1.077) = 0.430$, implying a net of tax rate of 0.570.

Consider next the value of $dt_a/d(1 - t)$, the ratio of the change in the average tax rate to the change in the marginal tax rate. For an individual with taxable income at exactly $140,000, the 1993 tax rates increased the marginal tax rate from 0.31 to 0.36 but left the tax liability and therefore the average tax rate unchanged. For such an individual, $dt_a/d(1 - t) = 0$, and there is no income effect. At incomes between $140,000 and $250,000, the average tax rate increases by 0.05 times the ratio of the taxable income above $140,000 to total taxable income. In this range, therefore, $dt_a/d(1 - t)$ is equal to the ratio of taxable income above $140,000 to total taxable income. At a taxable income of $250,000 the marginal tax rate jumps from 36 to 39.6 percent, temporarily reducing $dt_a/d(1 - t)$. After that, the ratio rises again toward a limiting value of 1.0.

We calculated the value of $(1 - t)[dt_a/d(1 - t)]$ for each taxpayer, multiplied that amount by $-dTI/dy = 0.37$, and added the estimate of the uncompensated elasticity $\eta = 0.66$ to obtain an estimate of the compensated elasticity for that taxpayer. The weighted average of these compensated elasticities, weighting by the projected 1993 ATI for that individual, is $\epsilon = 0.74$.

This weighted-average compensated elasticity for high-income taxpayers implied by the 1993 experience seems quite consistent with the compensated elasticity found by Feldstein (1995a) and by Auten and Carroll (1994) on the basis of the experience of a large panel of taxpayers before and after the 1986 tax cuts. The estimate preferred by Feldstein was 1.04, whereas the Auten–Carroll estimate was 1.33. The lower value of the current estimate of 0.74 may reflect the short-run nature of the observation for 1993, since the observed behavior refers to the same year in which the tax rate was changed. We return to this issue in Section 7.

6. THE DEADWEIGHT LOSS OF THE 1993 INCREASE IN PERSONAL TAX RATES

The compensated elasticities ϵ_{TI} calculated for each type of income of each taxpayer according to equation (6) can be used to estimate the deadweight loss for that taxpayer of increasing the marginal personal income tax rates from 31 to 36 and 39.6 percent. In this calculation, the marginal tax rate also includes the marginal payroll tax rate (if any).[29] For example, an individual with taxable compensation between $57,600 and $135,000 who is part of a taxpaying unit with total taxable income between $140,000 and $250,000 experiences a marginal tax rate increase on that income from $(0.31 + 0.029)/(1.0145) = 0.334$ to $(0.36 + 0.029)/(1.0145) = 0.383$.

When the increased deadweight losses are aggregated over all the individuals we obtain a total increase in the deadweight loss due to the 1993 increase in personal income tax rates of $15.9 billion.[30] This estimated increase in deadweight loss is thus nearly twice the estimated increase in tax revenue. Stated differently, for every dollar that the government collects as a result of the increase in the top personal income tax rates, the taxpayers incur a total cost of nearly $3—the dollar transferred to the government plus the deadweight loss of nearly $2.

The structure of the 1993 tax increase thus made it a very inefficient way of increasing revenue.

7. THE EFFECTS OF THE INCREASE ON THE HOSPITAL INSURANCE (HI) TAX BASE

Although elimination of the $135,000 ceiling on the HI tax base was enacted at the same time as the increase in personal income tax rates, it only took effect in January 1994. Our evidence therefore does not relate

---

[29] We use the expression in equation (4) to calculate the increased deadweight loss due to the change in the tax on each particular type of income. As noted earlier, we make no allowance for cross-price effects. We calculate each deadweight loss separately and then add them.

[30] Of this $15.9 billion, more than 70 percent ($11.4 billion) is associated with the increase from 31 to 39.6 percent. Of this $11.4 billion, very little involves marginal payroll tax rates; $6.4 billion is associated with compensation over $135,000, and $3.7 billion is associated with noncompensation income. In contrast, of the $3.9 billion increase in the deadweight loss associated with the rise in the marginal tax rate from 31 to 36 percent, $3.0 billion is associated with income that is subject to a marginal payroll tax rate at 2.9 percent ($2.2 billion) or 15.3 percent ($0.8 billion).

to the effect of that part of the tax increase.[31] We can, however, use our estimated elasticities to calculate the likely effect of the increased HI tax on tax revenue and on the deadweight loss.

Consider first the ways in which eliminating the ceiling on the HI tax base changes total tax revenue. Because the higher marginal tax rate causes a decline in taxable income, the additional HI tax is less than the amount that would have been collected if there were no behavioral response. More important, however, the decline in taxable income also reduces the income subject to the personal income tax and therefore reduces the personal income tax revenue.

These effects can be illustrated with the example of an individual who, with the behavior induced by the 1993 marginal tax rates, would have taxable income of $220,000 in 1993 and taxable compensation of $200,000.[32] Under the 1993 tax rules, that individual faced a marginal personal income tax rate of 36 percent and no marginal payroll tax. Under the 1994 tax rules, the individual would also face a combined employer–employee payroll tax of 2.9 percent, implying that the tax as a percentage of the individual's marginal product rises from 0.36 to $0.389/(1.0145) = 0.383$. The net of tax rate thus falls from 0.64 to 0.617, a decline of 3.6 percent. The estimated uncompensated elasticity of $\eta = 0.66$ implies that the individual's taxable income declines by 2.4 percent, from $220,000 to $214,720. If the compensation portion declines in the same proportion, taxable compensation falls from $200,000 to $195,200. The additional HI tax is 2.9 percent of the difference between $195,200 and $135,000, or $1,745. But the induced decline in taxable income of $5,280 (from $220,000 to $214,720) reduces personal tax collections at a 36 percent rate (i.e., by $1,901). For this taxpayer, the increase in the HI tax base actually reduces total tax payments by $156.

At higher incomes, the extra payroll tax can outweigh the loss of personal tax revenue. Consider, for example, a taxpayer with a taxable income of $330,000 and taxable compensation of $300,000. Under the 1993 tax rules, that individual faced a marginal personal income tax rate of 39.6 percent and no marginal payroll tax rate. Under the 1994 tax rules, the individual would also face a combined employer–employee payroll tax of 2.9 percent, implying that the tax as a percentage of the

---

[31] As previously noted, our analysis ignored the fact that taxpayers who were aware that the HI tax would increase in 1994 had an incentive to advance income into 1993. This causes us to underestimate the uncompensated and compensated elasticities.

[32] The difference between taxable income and taxable compensation is the difference between nonlabor income and itemized deductions.

individual's marginal product rises from 0.396 to 0.425/(1.0145) = 0.419. The net of tax rate thus falls from 0.604 to 0.581, a decline of 3.8 percent. The estimated uncompensated elasticity of $\eta = 0.66$ implies that the individual's taxable income declines by 2.51 percent, from $330,000 to $324,720. If the compensation portion declines in the same proportion, taxable compensation falls from $300,000 to $292,470. The additional HI tax is 2.9 percent of the difference between $292,470 and $135,000, or $4,566. But the induced decline in taxable income of $8,280 (from $330,000 to $321,720) reduces personal tax collections at a 39.6 percent rate (i.e., by $3,278). For this taxpayer, the increase in the HI tax increases total tax collection by only $1,288, or only 27 percent of the static revenue estimate of 2.9 percent of the $165,000 increased tax base at the initial level of compensation.

In the aggregate, we estimate that eliminating the $135,000 ceiling on the HI tax base reduced the predicted revenue (at 1993 income levels) from $2.1 billion with no behavioral response to only $600 million if taxpayers reduced their compensation (i.e., total wage and salary income plus schedule C income) in the same proportion that the 1993 experience implied for total taxable income. Only when the data for 1994 become available will it be possible to calculate the actual 1994 revenue response.

The Deadweight Loss of the Increased Hospital Insurance (HI) Tax Base

Consider next the deadweight loss caused by raising the level of income subject to the HI tax. There is of course no change in the deadweight loss for those categories of income that experience no change in the HI tax. This includes the compensation earned by individuals with compensation under $135,000 as well as all nonlabor income.[33] The deadweight loss needs to be evaluated only for individuals with taxable compensation over $135,000. There are two cases within this group: those with 1993 marginal tax rates of 36 percent and those with 1993 marginal tax rates of 39.6 percent. For each taxpayer, we evaluate the change in deadweight loss if the tax rate on compensation increases from 0.36 to 0.389/1.0145 = 0.383 or, for higher income taxpayers, from 0.396 to 0.425/1.0145 = 0.419.

The two cases discussed earlier in this section illustrate the nature of the calculation. For the taxpayer with $220,000 of taxable income and $200,000 of taxable compensation at 1993 rates, only the $200,000 is

---

[33] In calculating the deadweight loss of the increased tax on compensation, we ignore any possible compensated cross-price effects and therefore look only at the effect of the increased marginal tax rate on the behavior of that type of income.

relevant for evaluating the deadweight loss of the increase in the HI ceiling. Equation (4) implies that the increased deadweight loss for this individual is

$$\Delta\text{DWL} = 0.5\epsilon_{\text{TLI}}\{[(0.383)^2 - (0.360)^2]/[1 - 0.360]\}200,000$$
$$= 2,680\epsilon_{\text{TLI}}, \tag{7}$$

where ϵ_{TLI} is the elasticity of taxable labor income to the net of tax rate for such compensation.

The value of ϵ_{TLI} is not likely to be the same as the taxable income elasticity ϵ_{TI} because changes in the payroll tax rate do not provide any incentive to change deductions. To evaluate ϵ_{TLI} it is useful to consider first the corresponding uncompensated elasticity of taxable labor income with respect to the corresponding net of tax rate. The elasticity of overall taxable income with respect to the net of tax rate ($\eta = 0.66$) reflects the effect of the tax on labor supply, on the form of labor compensation (fringe benefits and working conditions versus cash) and on the use of deductibles. The elasticity of taxable compensation, which we label η_{TLI}, includes the first two of these but does not include the use of deductibles. It also includes an additional component: the substitution between taxable labor income and other forms of income. The 2.9 percent payroll tax gives individuals an incentive to shift income from taxable compensation to investment income. Although such a substitution may not be possible for most taxpayers, high-income individuals that are our focus here may be able to shift the form of compensation from labor income to rent, royalties, stock options, capital gains, etc. It is difficult to know the magnitude of this compensation–noncompensation substitution relative to the effect of the income tax on the use of itemized deductions. The difference may cause either a rise or a fall in going from the elasticity of taxable income to the elasticity of taxable labor income. To be very conservative, we shall set $\eta_{\text{TLI}} = 0.50$, approximately two thirds of the estimated elasticity of taxable income. We recognize that this is only an educated guess, but we think it is likely to be a conservative one.

The same analysis of income and substitution effects that led to equation (6) implies that

$$\eta_{\text{TLI}} = \epsilon_{\text{TLI}} + (1 - t)[dt_a/d(1 - t)](d\text{TLI}/dy). \tag{8}$$

For the individual with taxable compensation of $220,000 and taxable labor income of $200,000, the initial marginal tax rate is 36 percent, implying that $(1 - t) = 0.64$. Since the payroll tax increase is at a constant rate above the $135,000 threshold, the ratio $dt_a/d(1-t)$ is the ratio of the newly taxable compensation (in this case, $200,000 − $135,000 = $65,000) to total compensation: $(dt_a/d(1-t)) = 0.325$. The value of $dTLI/dy$ is the effect on taxable labor income of an increase in exogenous income. Omitting the decline in deductible expenditures (dD/dy that represented 0.071 of the estimated value of $dTI/dy = -0.37$) leaves the effect of exogenous income on the consumption of leisure and on the use of excludable income like fringe benefits. Unlike the substitution effect, there is no reason why an exogenous income increase should induce a change from taxable labor income to nonlabor income. We therefore take $dTLI/dy = -0.30$.

Substituting these estimates into equation (8) implies $\epsilon_{TLI} = \eta_{TLI} + 0.66(0.325)(0.30) = \eta_{TLI} + 0.06 = 0.56$. Equation (7) implies that the deadweight loss of the HI increase for this taxpayer is $1,501. Thus, the government collects $316 less in revenue with than without the higher HI tax but imposes a deadweight loss of $1,501.

Consider next the example of the higher compensation taxpayer with $300,000. The deadweight loss is based on increasing the marginal tax rate from 0.396 to 0.419:

$$\Delta DWL = 0.5\ \epsilon_{TLI}\{[(0.419)^2 - (0.396)^2]/(1 - 0.396)\}300,000$$
$$= 4,665\epsilon_{TLI} \qquad (9)$$

In this case, equation (8) implies that $\epsilon_{TLI} = 0.60$. The deadweight loss is therefore $2,799 whereas the increase in revenue is only $966. The total burden is thus nearly four times as much as the revenue raised.

We have calculated the increased deadweight loss for each of the affected taxpayers. The aggregate amount of the deadweight loss is $2.1 billion or more than three times the $600 million net revenue gain from eliminating the ceiling on the HI tax base.

8. POTENTIAL BIASES IN THE ESTIMATED TAXPAYER RESPONSE

In interpreting these results and comparing them with the earlier studies of the effects of the tax rate reductions in the 1980s, several potential sources of statistical bias should be borne in mind. Some of these cause our estimates to overstate the true long-term effect of the change in tax rates, whereas others cause our estimates to understate that true effect. This section discusses those biases and the future research that may help to resolve the resulting uncertainty as better data become available.

8.1 Short-Run Response

First, the current analysis refers to the changes in taxpayer behavior during the same year that Congress enacted the change in tax rates. Because it takes time for taxpayers to alter their behavior in response to the higher tax rates, our estimated first-year response may understate the longer term effect of the tax rate increases.[34] This longer term effect might, for example, involve changing jobs or employers, resulting in a more pleasant life-style but lower cash income. If this type of change is more pronounced among younger individuals who are still making career choices, it will affect the population as a whole only gradually. Similarly, older individuals may respond to the higher tax rates by advancing the date of their retirement or by choosing a mix of more retirement and less work. Again, it takes time before such decisions, made in a relatively narrow range of years, come to have a significant effect on the activity of a large segment of the labor force. All of these considerations suggest that the long-run effect will be greater than the short-run effect that has been observed in the present study. A similar difference may also apply to changes in deductions (e.g., the size of a mortgage or the purchase of a second home) and in exclusions (the employer's provision of more fringe benefits instead of larger increases in cash salaries.)

The observed same-year effect for 1993 may have been depressed further relative to the potential long-term effect by the fact that the legislation was not enacted until August of that year. Although the tax rate increases for high-income individuals were enacted as proposed in February 1993, other aspects of the President's tax plan were radically changed. Many taxpayers may therefore have waited until after August to begin changing their behavior.

In contrast to the current paper, the earlier studies of the effects of lower tax rates generally were based on taxpayer behavior two years or more after the tax cut. It is not surprising, therefore, that the estimated elasticities in the current study are substantially less than the elasticities estimated for the 1981 and 1986 tax rate reductions.

We will be able to remedy this problem when we have data for a longer period of time after 1993. For the reasons discussed later in this section, panel data through 1995 will be particularly valuable in estimating the longer-term response.

---

[34] The Treasury Department's estimates assume that the behavioral responses in the narrow range of changes that they consider do increase from a 7 percent revenue loss in the first year to a long-run behavioral response that reduces revenue by 16 percent in year 5 and beyond (see Auten and Carroll, 1994b).

8.2 Shifting of Income from 1993 to 1992

A second potential source of statistical bias could result from shifts of bonuses and other income from 1993 to 1992. Taxpayers who anticipated the 1993 tax increase may have taken steps to shift income from 1993 to 1992. The Treasury Department, in commenting on an earlier draft of our study, pointed to a Department of Commerce estimate that $20 billion of wage and salary income (including bonuses) was shifted from the first quarter of 1993 to the final quarter of 1992 and argued that our statistical estimate of a $29 billion loss of taxable income could be explained by such a one-time shift on the assumption that virtually all the income shifting was among taxpayers with an AGI greater than $200,000.

It is important to recognize, however, that because of our difference-in-difference method of estimation, a shift of income from 1993 to 1992 only biases our estimate of the tax-induced change in taxable income in this way if the intertemporal shift of income is a larger share of taxable income among the taxpayers in the $200,000-plus AGI group than among taxpayers in the $50,000 to $200,000 reference group. There is unfortunately no evidence on the distribution of income shifting. Moreover, wage and salary income constitutes only about two thirds of total taxable income among the top group but is actually equal to about 120 percent of taxable income among those in the reference group (because their adjustments and deductions exceed their nonwage incomes.) This implies that an intertemporal shift of income that was the same fraction of wages in the two groups would cause the rise in taxable income among the high-income group to be substantially greater than among the reference group. In that case, the income shifting would cause our difference-in-difference procedure to underestimate the true effect of the higher tax rates. Indeed, unless the relative wage shift was at least 80 percent higher among the top AGI group than among the reference group, the shifting would cause our estimate to understate the true effect of higher tax rates.

Although the top income group had a greater incentive to shift incomes, many in the reference group believed that they also had reason to shift income. As the 1994 *Economic Report of the President* notes, as late as July 1993 over 70 percent of respondents to a *Wall Street Journal*/NBC poll thought that middle-class taxpayers would bear most of the tax increases (p. 74).

There is of course some doubt about the accuracy of the estimated $20 billion of aggregate shifting. The $20 billion shift of wage and salary income from the first quarter of 1993 to the final quarter of 1992 is reported in the national income accounts as $20 billion of "wage accruals less disbursements." This is the only time (at least in the past 25 years for which we have data) in which the Commerce Department estimates a wage accruals less disbursements in excess of $1 billion. The staff of the Bureau of Economic Analysis (BEA) explain in the August 1993 *Survey of Current Business* (p. 28) that the method of estimating annual wage and salary accruals was changed for 1992 to reflect the possibility of a large amount of bonuses paid in 1992. This change was made because in early 1993, "reports indicated that bonus payments earned by many employees in the securities industry in 1992 that typically would have been paid in early 1993 had instead been paid in late 1992." The BEA initially estimated that $1.5 billion in bonus payments had been accelerated from 1993 to 1992. Later, on the basis of a comparison of the quarterly unemployment insurance reports of covered wages for the fourth quarter of 1992 with the corresponding fourth-quarter reports for the prior years back to 1982, the BEA revised its estimate and "concluded that about $20 billion" of fourth-quarter 1992 wage and salary income represented an acceleration of bonus payments from early 1993. This assumption was used by the BEA to estimate that the "wage accruals less disbursements" figure for the first quarter of 1993 was a negative $20 billion.

Estimating the extent of wage and salary shifting in the fourth quarter of 1992 is difficult because that quarter saw a quite dramatic surge of GDP. The rise in nominal GDP jumped from an annual rate of 4.9 percent in the third quarter of 1992 to 8.6 percent in the fourth quarter and then fell back again to 4.4 percent in the first quarter of 1993. Shifts in the timing of compensation would not affect these GDP estimates, since any shift in wage payments would cause a corresponding shift in profits. Since wage and salary payments are about half of GDP, a 4.9 percent increase would correspond to about $150 billion, whereas an 8.6 percent increase would correspond to about $260 billion. Deciding how much of the observed $125 billion increase in wage disbursements (seasonally adjusted) between the third and fourth quarters of 1992 was a "shift in timing" and how much was a result of the economic surge is a very difficult judgement to make.

We have, however, followed the procedure described by the BEA and examined the fourth quarter through insurance reports on covered wage and salary payments from 1982 to 1992. The fourth quarter of 1992 shows a substantial jump in reported wage and salary income, from the roughly $65 billion increase in the previous two years to a $106 billion increase in 1992. Again, it is difficult to know how much of this is due to the fact that nominal GDP rose at 8.6 percent in the fourth quarter of 1992 but at only 2.6 percent in the fourth quarter of 1991 and 0.5 percent in the fourth quarter of 1990.

We were also encouraged by the Treasury Department to examine the evidence on the change in income tax withholding between the end of 1992 and the beginning of 1993 that is published in the monthly *Treasury Bulletins*. Although the data are available monthly, the number of working days and the number of pay periods varies from month to month and year to year. We have therefore examined quarterly data on tax withholding. Between the fourth quarter of 1992 and the first quarter of 1993, tax withholding fell by $6.2 billion. However, there was an equally large drop a year later (a $6.2 billion decline in tax withholding between the final quarter of 1993 and the first quarter of 1994) and a decline that was almost as large in the previous year (a decline on $4.0 billion from the first quarter of 1991 to the first quarter of 1992). It is hard to conclude from the Treasury data that anything unusual occurred at the end of 1992.

8.3 Shifting of Income from 1994 to 1993

High-income taxpayers also had an incentive to shift income from 1994 to 1993. To the extent that such shifting occurred and that it was relatively greater than the shifting among those in the $50,000 to $200,000 AGI class, our estimates would understate the effect of the 1993 tax rate increases.

One reason for the high-income taxpayers to shift income from 1994 to 1993 was to avoid the 2.9 percent payroll tax scheduled to begin in January 1994. For a taxpayer with a 39.6 percent marginal rate of personal income tax, eliminating the ceiling on income subject to the HI tax raised the marginal tax rate to 41.9 percent. The net tax share thus decreased by 3.8 percent.

There was, moreover, substantial uncertainty even in 1993 about whether the Administration's proposal would be enacted and, if enacted, whether it would be "retroactive" to January 1993. Many high-income taxpayers hoped that tax rates for 1993 would be increased only part of the way to the full higher rates that would begin in 1994. Those who thought that there was some possibility that the rates would be lower in 1993 than in 1994 had an incentive to advance from future years to 1993 (e.g., by shifting a bonus from 1994 to 1993 or by ending a deferred compensation arrangement).

The change in the alternative minimum tax provided another reason why some taxpayers might have shifted some income from 1994 to 1993. The AMT raises an individual's overall tax liability by eliminating deductions and adjustments to income that would be allowed under the ordinary income tax but taxes that greater income at a lower marginal rate than the ordinary income tax. The current AMT rate is 26 percent. An individual who faced the AMT in 1993 but expected to avoid the AMT in 1994 would have an incentive to shift compensation from 1994 to 1993 to take advantage of the lower overall tax rate.

Although the official estimates of "wage accruals less disbursements" show no unusual activity at the end of 1993, the underlying evidence used by the BEA to impute a $20 billion value of "wage accruals less disbursements" to the final quarter of 1992 suggests an approximately equally large adjustment for the final quarter of 1993. We have already noted that the Treasury withholding receipts fell by exactly the same amount from the end of 1993 to start of 1994 as it did between the end of 1992 and the first quarter of 1993. In addition, the wages covered by unemployment insurance reported for the fourth quarter of 1993 also jumped by a large $97 billion (similar to the $106 billion in the final quarter of 1992) before reverting to $64 billion in the final quarter of 1994, the same level that had prevailed in the final quarters of 1990 and 1991.

It is impossible to use the currently available tax data itself to sort out the role of shifting versus sustained taxable changes in taxable income. Only when panel data through 1995 become available will it be possible to address this issue in a fully satisfactory way.

8.4 Assuming No Tax Increases in the $50,000 to $200,000 AGI Reference Group

The difference-in-difference method assumes that the tax rates increased among those with AGIs greater than $200,000 but that there were no tax rate increases in the reference group with AGIs between $50,000 and $200,000. In fact, some taxpayers in this reference group (about 3 percent overall and 10 percent among those with AGIs between $100,000 and $200,000) did have incomes high enough to make them subject to the 1993 rise in tax rates. This "contamination" of the reference group means that the assumed change in tax rates between the two groups is larger than the actual one. This in turn causes an underestimate of the sensitivity of taxable income to the rise in tax rates and a corresponding underestimate of the implied elasticity.

8.5 Lack of Panel Data

The current study is not based on actual panel data that would allow following the same individuals through time as tax rates change. Although the earlier studies of the 1986 tax reductions using panel data were consistent with previous studies using the current type of "synthetic" panel data, the lack of actual panel data does introduce additional uncertainty in the estimates. The individuals in the highest income group are not the same in 1993 and 1992, a problem that is compounded by the fact that AGI includes capital gains, whereas our focus is on the taxable income excluding capital gains. Moreover, the reference group is necessarily defined in terms of nominal income levels rather than real income levels or equal numbers of taxpayers. We do not see any reason why this should bias the results but recognize that it does introduce additional uncertainty that would not be present with panel data.

The problem of comparing groups in different years becomes greater as the time between the years increases. For that reason, we were reluctant to extend our analysis from the comparison of 1993 and 1992 to earlier years. We did, however, repeat our analysis using 1991 as a reference year. More specifically, we used the change in taxable incomes between 1991 and 1993 in the group with nominal AGIs of $50,000 to $200,000 as the standard for predicting the rise in taxable incomes among those with AGIs over $200,000. Unlike the 1992-based comparison, the 1991-based comparison showed no tendency to overestimate the taxable income of the high-income group. There is no way to know whether this reflects the statistical biases associated with income shifting, the reduced comparability of taxpayers in the same AGI groups when we go from one year to two based on nominal income classification, or the very strong business cycle recovery that occurred in 1991. Only good panel data from 1991 through 1995 will be able to provide a fully reliable answer to this question.

8.6 Assuming a Stable Income Distribution

The difference-in-difference approach implicitly assumes that the relative rates of increase of taxable incomes would have been the same in the high-income and reference groups if there had been no change in tax rates. A substantial amount of evidence suggests that higher incomes are in fact rising more rapidly. Although some of this may itself be tax induced, there is substantial evidence that higher incomes are rising more rapidly than lower incomes for nontax reasons as well.

To the extent that the high-income taxpayers would have had greater income increases than taxpayers in the reference group in the absence of a tax change, our difference-in-difference method causes us to underestimate the true effect of the rise in tax rates. It would be desirable to try to estimate the extent of the likely change in income distribution due to nontax factors. This, too, will be helped when we have data that extends to at least 1995, since that eliminates any possible distortions due to temporary income shifting between 1993 and 1994. It would be desirable also to analyze this in a way that separates cyclical influence on the income distribution.

9. CONCLUSIONS AND CAVEATS

Several tentative conclusions emerge from this study. First, the basic estimates suggest that taxpayers reduced their taxable incomes in response to the higher 1993 marginal tax rates. Although the reductions were not absolutely large, they were large enough to imply a loss of about half of the additional revenue that would have been raised by the 1993 tax rate increases if there had been no behavioral response.

Second, the implied elasticities are somewhat lower than the sensitivity reported in previous studies of the response to the tax rate decreases of the 1980s. This may reflect the fact that the current estimates relate to the taxpayer responses within the same year that the tax rate was enacted and that the legislation was enacted only in August of the year.

Third, the estimates imply that the structure of the 1993 tax rate increase resulted in very little net revenue despite the sharp increase in marginal tax rates. The estimated taxpayer response implies a loss of more than half of the additional personal income tax revenue that would have occurred with no behavioral response. The reduction in payroll tax revenue that resulted from reduced incomes increased the overall leakage of tax revenue to 5.7 percent of the static estimate. Instead of raising $19.3 billion of additional personal income tax revenue, the higher marginal tax rates led to an estimated revenue increase of only $8.4 billion. These estimates differ very greatly from the traditional and virtually "static" revenue estimates used by the Treasury Department and the Congressional Joint Tax Committee.[35]

Fourth, the behavioral response implies a compensated elasticity that is about 0.74. This in turn implies that increasing marginal tax rates from 31 to 36 and 39.6 percent raised the deadweight loss of the personal income tax by $15.9 billion. Thus, the 1993 personal tax rate increases raised the deadweight loss by approximately $2 for every additional dollar of tax revenue.

Finally, we used the estimated response to the higher personal income tax rates in 1993 to evaluate the effect of the increase in the HI tax base that took effect in January 1994. The combined employer–employee tax of 2.9 percent raised payroll tax revenue of about $2.0 billion. But the higher marginal tax rates that resulted are likely to have caused a decline in personal income tax revenue of $1.4 billion. The net effect of eliminat-

---

[35] Recall that the Treasury Department assumed that the revenue loss due to taxpayer responses would be only 7 percent of the static no-behavioral-response revenue (Auten and Carroll, 1995).

ing the $135,000 ceiling on the HI tax base was therefore to raise total federal tax revenue by only $600 million.

Several possible statistical biases could cause the estimated effect of the tax changes to either underestimate or overestimate the true long-run effects. These were discussed in Section 8. Only further research, preferably with panel data for a longer period of time, can resolve some of these uncertainties. But until these additional studies are done, it seems reasonable to conclude that the higher marginal tax rates in 1993 raised substantially less revenue than a static estimate would imply and imposed relatively large deadweight losses.

REFERENCES

Auerbach, Alan (1994). "The U.S. Fiscal Problem: Where We Are, How We Got Here, and Where We're Going." in *NBER Macroeconomics Annual 1994*, Stanley Fischer and Julio Rotemberg (eds.). Cambridge, MA: The MIT Press, pp. 141–175.

———. (1995). "Tax Projections and the Budget: Lessons from the 1980s." *American Economic Review* 85(no. 2, May): 165–169.

Auten, Gerald, and Robert Carroll (1995). "Behavior of the Affluent and the 1986 Tax Reform Act." In *Proceedings of the Eighty-Seventh Annual Conference on Taxation of the National Tax Association*, Columbus, Ohio: 70–76.

———. (1994). "Tax Rates, Taxpayer Behavior and the 1993 Act." In *Proceedings of the Eighty-Sixth Annual Conference of the National Tax Association*, Columbus, Ohio: 7–12.

Bureau of Economic Analysis, *Survey of Current Business*, August, 1993, p. 23.

Council of Economic Advisors, *The Economic Report of the President*, 1995. February 1995, GPO, Washington, D.C.

Cruciano, Teresa (1995). "Individual Income Tax Returns, Preliminary Data, 1993." *Statistics of Income Bulletin*. Washington, DC: U.S. Department of Treasury, Internal Revenue Service, Summer.

Eissa, Nada (1995). "Taxation and Labor Supply of Married Women: The Tax Reform Act of 1986 as a Natural Experiment." NBER Working Paper no. 5023, February.

———. (1996). "Labor Supply and the Economic Recovery Act of 1981." Forthcoming in *Empirical Foundations of Household Taxation*, Martin Feldstein and James Poterba (eds.).

Feenberg, Daniel, and James Poterba (1993). "Income Inequality and the Incomes of Very High Income Taxpayers." In *Tax Policy and the Economy*, Vol. 7, James Poterba (ed.). Cambridge, MA: The MIT Press.

Feldstein, Martin (1994). "The Case for Dynamic Analysis." *Wall Street Journal* December 14.

———. (1995a). "The Effect of Marginal Tax Rates on Taxable Income: A Panel Study of the 1986 Tax Reform Act." *Journal of Political Economy*, vol. 103, no. 3, pp. 551–572, June.

———. (1995b). "Behavioral Responses to Tax Rates: Evidence from TRA86." *American Economic Review* 85(no. 2, May), pp. 170–174, AEA Papers and Proceedings.

———. (1995c). "Tax Avoidance and the Deadweight Loss of the Income Tax." NBER Working Paper no. 5055.

———, and Daniel Feenberg (1993). "Higher Tax Rates with Little Revenue Gain: An Empirical Analysis of the Clinton Tax Plan." *Tax Notes,* vol. 58, no. 12, pp. 1653–1657, March 22.

———. (1995). "The Taxation of Two Earner Families." NBER Working Paper no. 5155, June. Forthcoming in *Empirical Foundations of Household Taxation,* Martin Feldstein and James Poterba, (eds.).

Lindsey, Lawrence (1987). "Individual Taxpayer Response To Tax Cuts: 1982–1984, with Implications for the Revenue Maximizing Tax Rate." *Journal of Public Economics* 33: 173–206.

Navratil, John (1995). "Essay on the Impact of Marginal Tax Rate Reductions on the Reporting of Taxable Income on Individual Income Tax Returns." Doctoral Dissertation, Harvard University.

U.S. Treasury, U.S. Treasury Bulletin, various issues, 1979–1995.

TAX REFORMS AND LABOR SUPPLY

Nada Eissa
University of California–Berkeley and NBER

The 1980s were a period of substantial changes in the U.S. tax code and income distribution. Even after controlling for demand-side factors that altered the returns to education, researchers have shown that behavioral responses to tax reform remain substantial. This paper reviews the lessons that have emerged from research on the behavioral response to tax reforms, focusing primarily on the labor supply response. The paper also builds on that work by examining whether the dramatic responses in taxable income over the 1980s are due to an increase in male labor market participation. Microdata from 1976 to 1993 are consistent with only a small male labor supply response after the Tax Reform Act of 1986. This finding is important for the interpretation of previous work and for the design of tax policy.

1. INTRODUCTION

The 1980s were a period of substantial changes in the U.S. tax code. Between 1980 and 1989, two tax laws collapsed the federal personal income tax schedule from 14 to 2 (nominal) brackets,[1] reduced the top

---

This paper was prepared for the 1995 National Bureau of Economic Research Conference on Tax Policy and the Economy, Washington, D.C., November 7. I thank Doug Elmendorf and Jim Poterba for helpful comments on an earlier draft and Mark Rodini and Jimmy Torrez for research assistance. The Institute of Business and Economic Research at the University of California–Berkeley provided financial support.

[1] The phaseout of the personal exemption and the 15 percent bracket created additional 33 percent brackets for upper income taxpayers.

marginal rate from 70 to 28 percent, and removed an estimated 6 million poor households from the tax rolls. For the typical family with twice the median income, the marginal rate on income was 15 percentage points lower in 1988 than in 1980. For the family with the median income, the federal marginal rate was 9 percentage points lower (see Bosworth and Burtless, 1992).

The 1980s were also a period of substantial changes in the income distribution. Between 1980 and 1990, the share of income accruing to the top 5 percent of the family income distribution rose from 15.3 to 17.4 percent. The share of income accruing to the top quintile of that income distribution rose from 41.5 to 44.3 percent. Many explanations for the rising share of income at the top of the distribution have been put forward, mostly related to changes in the returns to education that derive from the demand side of the market. Even after controlling for other factors, several researchers (Lindsey, 1987; Feldstein, 1995; Navratil, 1994; Auten and Carroll, 1995) have shown that behavioral responses to tax reform are part of the explanation for the rising share of income at the top of the distribution.[2]

This paper reviews the evidence on the behavioral response to the tax reforms, focusing primarily on the labor supply response. Several studies provide direct evidence on the labor supply response (Bosworth and Burtless, 1992; Eissa, 1995a,b; Eissa and Liebman, 1995). The studies that look at the taxable response, on the other hand, provide suggestive evidence of labor supply responses. Although that evidence shows that growth in wage and salary income is an important component of the taxable income response (Navratil, 1994; Slemrod, 1995), it does not separate the labor supply response from other factors, such as reporting and compensation decisions.

Although the female labor supply did respond to the incentives in the tax reforms, it is unlikely that the increase in income is due to their increasing labor market participation. Overall, the share of women in the work force increased by 3 percentage points between 1980 and 1990, from 42.4 to 45.4 percent, but unless married, these women are not at the upper end of the income distribution, where we observe most of the income responses. Moreover, women married to high-income men do not earn enough to explain the surge in income. Mean earnings of married women in the highest decile of the taxable income distribution were $5,100 in 1985 ($11,638 conditional on working) (Navratil, 1994).

Essentially all research shows that male participation and hours of

---

[2] The findings are derived from the distribution of taxable income, which can differ from the family income distribution.

work do not respond to changes in after-tax wages (Hausman, 1985; Pencavel, 1986; Triest, 1992). However, two reasons suggest that studying the male labor supply is important: first, the strong income response to the tax reforms in the 1980s raises the question of whether male labor market participation is an important component. Second, the participation decision of men may have become more responsive to taxes because their participation rate is much lower than it was two decades ago (Heckman, 1993). During 1967–1969, the participation rate of men was 92.7 percent, but by 1985–1987, it had fallen to 86.8 percent (Juhn, 1992).

This paper examines the labor supply response of prime-age men (between the ages of 16 and 48) to the tax reforms of the 1980s. Using microdata from 1976 to 1993 and estimating simple reduced-form labor supply regressions, I find results that are consistent with a small labor supply response to the tax reforms. For men with more than 16 years of schooling, the estimated increase in total hours of work is about 50 hours per year, or 2 percent. The estimates suggest that the income response observed in the tax return data is due more to other factors, such as shifting of income, other dimensions of labor supply (productivity, occupational choice), and compensation decisions.

The current paper is organized as follows. Section 2 describes important features of the U.S. tax reforms from 1980 to 1993 and covers changes in the taxation of earned income resulting from the Economic Recovery Tax Act of 1981 (ERTA), the Tax Reform Act of 1986 (TRA), and the Omnibus Budget Reconciliation Act of 1993 (OBRA93). Section 3 then reviews the evidence on the behavioral responses to taxes. An analysis of the male labor supply follows in Section 4, which covers the data and the results. Finally, Section 5 concludes the paper.

2. TAX REFORMS, 1980–1993

In this section, I summarize features of the tax laws that are relevant for the treatment of earned income. In addition to the three tax laws passed (ERTA, TRA, and OBRA93), changes in the social security system that affected marginal (and average) rates for many taxpayers are discussed.

The first major tax law of the period, the ERTA, was passed in 1981. The ERTA called for an across-the-board reduction in marginal tax rates of 23 percent, to be phased in between 1982 and 1984.[3] The top tax rate

---

[3] A secondary earner tax deduction, equal to 10 percent of the earnings of the lower earning spouse up to $30,000 was introduced. This provision is unlikely to affect the labor supply decisions of the primary earner (typically the husband) in the most basic labor supply model.

TABLE 1
Features of Federal Income Tax Code

	Gross income (1988$)	1970	1980	1985	1989	1993
Marginal tax rates by filing status						
Single	$10,000	19.5	18	11	15	15
	$20,000	22.6	26	23	15	15
Married, filing jointly[a]	$10,000	14	12.5	23.22	10	19.5
	$35,000	22.6	28	25	15	15
	$50,000	25.6	37	33	28	28
	$110,000	43.1	54	45	33	31
	$220,000	56.4	64	50	28	36
Top bracket		71.75	70	50	28	39.6
Social security						
Total payroll tax rate		8.80	12.26	14.10	15.02	15.02
Maximum taxable income		$7,800	$25,900	$39,600	$48,000	$50,600
EITC						
Phasein rate		0	10	11	14	19.5
Phaseout rate		0	12.5	12.22	10	13.93
Maximum eligible income		0	$10,000	$11,000	$19,340	$23,050

Sources: Statistics of Income (1993), Hausman and Poterba (1987), Pechman (1987), and Deloitte and Touche (1993).

[a] Assumed to have two dependents and only one spouse working.

EITC, earned income tax credit.

bracket was lowered from 70 to 50 percent, effective in 1982. The ERTA included few provisions to alter the tax base, and so lower marginal rates should have translated into lower average rates for these taxpayers.

Although the ERTA reduced statutory marginal rates within each bracket, this did not translate into lower effective marginal (and average) rates for many taxpayers. For high-income taxpayers, the effective reduction in marginal rates was less than the implied 20 percentage points because the Maximum Tax, passed as part of the Tax Reform Act of 1969, kept marginal rates on earned income well below the 70 percent rate (see Lindsey, 1981). For many low- and middle-income taxpayers, marginal (and average) rates did not fall because of the increase in social security taxes. The payroll tax (on the employer and the employee) was increased by 2.76 percentage points, and the maximum taxable income was increased from $25,900 in 1980 to $39,600 in 1985 (Table 1).[4] This offset a full percentage point of the marginal rate reduction for the taxpayer earning $35,000 after the ERTA.[5] Taxpayers with less than $50,000 faced the same or higher effective rates after the ERTA as before (Lindsey, 1987).

The TRA represented a shift in the tax code to low marginal rates imposed on a broad tax base. It was designed to be both revenue neutral and distributionally neutral. The tax law had important effects on low- and high-income taxpayers and little or no effect on a large section of the population. Hausman and Poterba (1987) estimate that more than 40 percent of the population would see a change in marginal rates of less than 10 percent, whereas only 11 percent would face marginal tax reductions of at least 10 percentage points.[6] The tax law collapsed the previous 11 income tax brackets into 2 (nominal) brackets: 15 and 28 percent. The

---

However, the deduction should generate some substitution in the labor supply of husband and wife if they make a joint decision.

[4] The appropriate social security tax is the difference between the present discounted value of benefits and the present discounted value of taxes. Although the difference is small for men (Feldstein and Samwick, 1992), the properly measured tax rate nonetheless increased during the decade.

[5] For some, the increase in the maximum taxable income raised marginal rates by the full 14 percentage points.

[6] To reconcile these figures with the data of Bosworth and Burtless cited previously, it is important to recognize that the effects of the TRA on marginal rates for taxpayers near the median of the income distribution are quite heterogeneous. The 15 percent bracket in 1989 included taxpayers who had faced marginal rates between 11 and 24 percent in 1980. The typical family with the median income in the study by Bosworth and Burtless faced a 24 percent rate in 1980 and a 15 percent rate in 1989. Taxpayers with slightly more income faced the 28 percent rate in 1980 and 1989. Hausman and Poterba (1987) present aggregate figures based on the distribution of taxpayers along the tax schedule.

phaseout of the 15 percent bracket and the personal exemption created a 33 percent tax bracket for higher income individuals.

For high-income individuals, the TRA reduced the top income marginal rate from 50 to 28 percent by 1988. Statutory marginal rates fell by at least 10 percentage points for those with taxable income over $65,000. The income effect of these marginal rate reductions was offset for higher income individuals by the expansion of the tax base. After the TRA, taxpayers could no longer exclude 60 percent of capital gains from adjusted gross income (AGI), deduct certain interest payments, or use passive losses to offset other income.[7]

For poor Americans, the law affected both average and marginal tax rates. It removed an estimated 6 million taxpayers from the tax rolls by increasing the dependent exemption (from $1,086 in 1986 to $1,950 in 1988) and the standard deduction (from $2,480 in 1986 to $4,400 in 1988 for a taxpayer filing as head of household). In addition, the Earned Income Tax Credit (EITC) was expanded. The EITC is a refundable credit, so taxpayers who owed no taxes could have received a refund of up to $874 in 1988.[8] The expansions in the EITC and other provisions in the TRA of 1986 reduced the tax liability for the average female head of household by $1,100 (Eissa and Liebman, 1995).

Although the Omnibus Budget Reconciliation Act of 1990 increased the top rate to 31 percent, by the early 1990s marginal rates on the highest income Americans were substantially lower than a decade earlier (see Table 1). Partially to redress the perceived inequities in the tax system due to the tax reforms of the 1980s, the OBRA93 included several provisions to increase the progressivity of the tax code. The OBRA93 increased marginal rates for high-income individuals. It created a new tax bracket, 36 percent for taxpayers earning over $140,000. Also, a surtax on individuals earning more than $250,000 effectively created a 39.6 percent bracket.[9]

---

[7] The TRA also increased the corporate income tax, generating additional income and substitution effects for some high-income individuals.

[8] The EITC creates a complicated and ambiguous set of labor supply incentives. Standard labor supply theory predicts that the EITC will encourage labor force participation because it is available only to taxpayers with earned income. But theory also predicts that the credit reduces the number of hours worked by most eligible taxpayers already in the labor force. Although the credit initially increases with income, producing offsetting income and substitution effects on hours worked, more than 70 percent of recipients have incomes in regions in which the credit is constant (and therefore produces only a negative income effect on labor supply) or is being phased out (producing negative income and substitution effects).

[9] Additional provisions in the OBRA93 raised the highest marginal rate even further. Taxpayers earning more than $108,450 were required to reduce their itemized deductions by 3 percent and thus faced a marginal rate of 41 percent. Also, the law adds another 2.9

The OBRA93 also expanded the EITC for low-income individuals. The expansions of the EITC are such that by 1996, it will surpass Aid to Families with Dependent Children (AFDC) as the largest federal program to alleviate poverty. The credit is scheduled to be phased in at a 40 percent rate up to a maximum of $3,370 for a family with two or more children and at a 34 percent rate for a family with one child up to a maximum of $2,040.

These tax reforms clearly generated both income and substitution effects. To consider their effects, we refer to the basic model generally used to analyze labor supply and taxes. The model hypothesizes that the individual maximizes utility to determine consumption (of a composite good) and hours of work. A tax increase makes the individual poorer and reduces his consumption of leisure (increases work). This is the *income effect*. A tax also reduces the after-tax wage and makes the individual work less. This is the *substitution effect*. Since these effects work in opposite directions, the net effect of tax reform on labor supply is usually ambiguous. Under some circumstances, the direction of the labor supply effect of a tax reform can be certain. A tax reform that reduces marginal rates but leaves average rates constant has an unambiguous positive effect on hours of work.

3. WHAT ACTUALLY HAPPENED: BEHAVIORAL RESPONSES TO TAX REFORMS

The tax reforms of the 1980s gave economists an unprecedented opportunity to study individual behavioral responses to taxes.[10] To study the

---

percent (on the employer and the employee) to the marginal rate for workers with wages and salary over $135,000 by eliminating the cap on the hospital insurance portion of social security.

[10] To place the following discussion in context, it is useful to consider the labor supply literature in the early 1980s and its implications for the effects of the tax reforms on labor supply. Since the labor supply literature is large and has been reviewed extensively elsewhere (see Hausman, 1985; Pencavel, 1986; Heckman and Killingsworth, 1986), the focus here is on research based on Hausman (1981). For a critique of the Hausman study, see MaCurdy, Green, and Paarsch (1990). Hausman estimated preference parameters by solving an optimizing model in which the nonlinear and nonconvex budget constraints facing the taxpayers are carefully modeled. Using maximum likelihood methods and cross-sectional data from the 1975 Panel Study of Income Dynamics (PSID), Hausman estimated total hour elasticities for married women and female heads of households similar to those in the literature at the time. For men, however, his estimates differed markedly. Although Hausman estimated an uncompensated elasticity of near zero for men, he found a large income effect and by definition a large substitution effect of taxes. The important implication of these estimates is that although the tax system does not affect hours worked, it affects economic welfare.

behavioral response to the tax reforms, researchers have used repeated cross sectional data (Lindsey, 1987; Feenberg and Poterba, 1993; Eissa, 1995a), aggregate time series data (Bosworth and Burtless, 1992; Slemrod 1995), and panel data (Feldstein, 1995; Navratil, 1994; Auten and Carroll, 1995). The story that emerges from this work is that behavioral responses to taxes are significant, especially for high-income individuals. In this section, I review the evidence on the response in labor supply and more generally in taxable income. A review of the taxable income response is important because it remains unexplained and raises the question of whether male labor supply is part of the response.

3.1 Total Labor Supply

Bosworth and Burtless (1992) were the first to study the labor supply response to the tax reforms of the 1980s directly. They used aggregate data from 1967 to 1989, which they generated from the Current Population Survey (CPS) to estimate time-series hours of work regressions. Their specification allowed two linear trends, one from 1967 to 1989 and another starting in 1981, and an adjustment for business cycle effects. Their regression estimates suggested that men worked 6 percent more hours and women 5.4 percent more hours in 1989 than in 1981.

To exploit the heterogeneous effect of the tax reforms on individuals, Bosworth and Burtless (1992) analyzed responses for individuals at different quintiles of the income distribution. They found that individuals in the bottom quintile increased their labor supply the most. They estimated a 31 and 16.7 percent increase in total hours worked by men and women, respectively, in the bottom quintile, but only a 3.2 and 11.8 percent increase by men and women in the top quintile. As they note, this pattern is not consistent with a pure labor supply story. Marginal and average rates remained largely unchanged for the bottom quintile, whereas they fell for the top quintile. Because the pattern of responses does not show that highest income individuals respond most, they concluded that their results only weakly support the prediction of a labor supply response.

However, the anomaly of large responses by men and women in the

---

Hausman (1981) used his estimates to simulate the labor supply effects of 10 and 30 percent reductions in marginal rates. He estimated that a 10 percent reduction in marginal rates would increase labor supply by 1.1 percent for men and 4.1 percent for women, whereas a 30 percent reduction would increase labor supply by 2.7 percent for men and 9.4 percent for women. The expectation in the early 1980s was that labor supply would increase substantially after the ERTA, which bracketed the Hausman simulations. Later in the decade, Hausman and Poterba (1987) also used the Hausman estimates to predict the effects of the TRA of 1986. They concluded that the TRA of 1986 would have only modest effects on aggregate labor supply because it had only modest effects on marginal rates.

bottom quintile may be partially explained by the business cycle. In 1981, the national unemployment rate was 7.6 percent. By 1989, it had fallen to 5.3 percent, the lowest rate since 1973. The bottom quintile of the family income distribution in 1981 will include a disproportionate number of individuals who are unemployed because of the recession. Although Bosworth and Burtless (1992) adjust for business cycle effects in their regressions, their procedure almost builds in a response after 1981. This built-in increase in labor supply by men in the bottom quintile results from depressing their total hours worked in 1981 by allocating to that group men who are strongly affected by the recession.

Another anomaly from the perspective of a tax response is that hours worked by older groups (between ages 45 and 64) increased at a faster rate after 1981 than hours worked by younger groups. However, labor market participation by older men may be responding to different factors, such as social security and private pensions. The large increase in the growth of social security benefits throughout the late 1960s and 1970s and the subsequent decline in the 1980s may explain part of the trend in the labor market participation of older men.

3.2 Female Labor Supply

In this section I review studies that focused on the female labor supply response to the tax reforms (Eissa, 1995a,b; Eissa and Liebman, 1995). Eissa (1995a,b) analyzed the effect of the TRA and ERTA on the labor supply of married women, and Eissa and Liebman (1995) analyzed the effect of the EITC and other provisions in the TRA on the labor supply of female heads of households.

These studies differ from Bosworth and Burtless (1992) in the data and methodology used. Although all the studies used the March CPS, Bosworth and Burtless (1992) used data from 1967 to 1989, whereas Eissa (1995a,b) and Eissa and Liebman (1995) used data immediately surrounding the actual tax acts. In addition, Bosworth and Burtless (1992) aggregated the data by demographic group, and so had a single annual observation for each group. Eissa (1995a,b) and Eissa and Liebman (1995), in contrast, used individual data. This strategy reflected the source of variation used to estimate the effect of the tax laws. By aggregating the data, Bosworth and Burtless (1992) relied on time to identify the effects of the tax laws. In their study, the change in the time trend starting in 1981 signaled the response to the tax reforms. The Eissa (1995a,b) and Eissa and Liebman (1995) studies, discussed in more detail in this section, relied on variation in marginal rates over time and between groups to identify the effect of the law.

The idea of these reports is that tax reforms offer time variation in marginal and average rates that is arguably more exogenous than is available in the cross section. Generally, cross-sectional labor supply equations are hard to estimate for reasons that relate to endogenous and missing wages, taxes, and nonlinear budget sets. The first problem is that taxes and labor supply are endogenously determined. A second problem is that cross-sectional differences in after-tax wages result from differences in education, family structure and size, and other factors that also affect labor supply decisions. A third problem encountered in the empirical analysis of taxation and labor supply is that nonlinear budget sets, owing to a progressive tax schedule, complicate the estimation procedure considerably.

To avoid these complications, these studies focused on groups that were strongly affected by the tax laws. To estimate the effect of the law, they compared the change in labor supply of women whose incentives were greatly affected with those whose incentives were little affected. For example, the TRA reduced marginal rates for women whose husbands were at the top of the income distribution but less so for those whose husbands were lower in the income distribution. The EITC, on the other hand, affected single women with qualifying children and did not affect single women without children.[11] The difference in the change in hours worked by these two groups is an estimate of the effect of the law.

The assumption that identifies the effect of the policy is that allocation to the treatment (affected) group is exogenous. If there were no assortative mating (people did not marry those who are like them), or if having a child were an exogenous event, this assumption would generate treatment and control groups that have the same distribution of preferences and characteristics. However, it is unlikely that any policy change would differentially affect otherwise identical groups. Women who marry upper income men are observationally different from women who marry lower income men. To overcome this problem, we control for relevant characteristics. Once observable characteristics are controlled for, the assumption is weakened substantially. To identify the response, we require that the distribution of unobservables remains constant over time.

To control for differences in the observable characteristics of the respective groups, Eissa (1995a,b) and Eissa and Liebman (1995) estimate equations of the following form:

---

[11] A qualifying child is a child, grandchild, stepchild, or foster child of the taxpayer; is under the age of 19 (under 24 if a full-time student) or permanently disabled; and has lived with the taxpayer for more than one half of the tax year.

$$l_{it} = f(\alpha_0 + \alpha_1 Q_{it} + \beta_0 I_j + \beta_1 I_t + \beta_2 I_{jt}), \tag{1}$$

where I_j is a dummy variable for the treatment group (and is zero for the control group); I_t is a dummy variable for time ($t = 1$ after the tax acts); I_{jt} is the product of the time and group dummy variables; Q includes observable characteristics of the individual; l_{it} is the measure of labor supply (participation and hours worked); and f is the normal density in the participation equation.

This "difference-in-difference" approach requires that there are no contemporaneous changes in policy or other factors that differentially affect the two groups. Where possible, one can account for such occurrences by changing the specification of Q. For example, high-income women have more education than low-income women at a time when returns to education were increasing. Such differences can bias the results because they conflate the effects of increased demand with responses to tax reductions. If Q includes a variable that interacts education with time, the bias is reduced.

Using imputed marginal tax rates, the elasticity of labor supply is calculated as follows:

$$\eta = \frac{\beta_2}{\Delta(1-\tau)^T - \Delta(1-\tau)^C}, \tag{2}$$

where β_2 is the difference in labor supply changes (see equation [1]); τ is the marginal rate; Δ is the percent change; T is the treatment group; and C is the control group.

3.2.1 Married Women Using data from the 1984–1986 and 1990–1992 March CPS, Eissa (1995a) identified the impact of tax reform by comparing the change in labor supplied by higher income women to the change in labor supplied by women with less income. Higher income women were those whose other household income (husband's earned income and family unearned income) placed them at or above the 99th percentile of the CPS income distribution; women with less income were between the 75th and 80th and the 90th and 95th percentiles of the same income distribution.

Table 2 presents the figures for the increase in labor force participation and in total labor supply under different assumptions. These figures are based on predictions from participation and hours-worked regressions, specified as equation (1). The top panel shows the relative increase in the labor force participation rate of high-income married women; the bottom

TABLE 2
Effects of TRA of 1986 on Labor Supply of High-Income Married Women and Their Elasticity Estimates

Control group	Raw data (%)	Demographic controls (%)	Adding education interaction (%)	Elasticity estimate
Participation response				
No control group	34.5			
75th percentile	12.3	8.4	4.3	0.2–0.4
90th percentile	13.0	10.9	11.4	0.6
Total labor supply				
No control group	19.5			
75th percentile	22.8	18.4	12.3	0.6–1.0
90th percentile	19.8	16.9	14.6	0.9–1.0

Data are March Current Population Survey 1984–1986 and 1990–1992; see Eissa (1995a) for details.

panel presents the corresponding figures for the increase in total hours of work per year. Although several estimates of the impact of the TRA are plausible, all point to the general conclusion that the labor supply of married women increased after the reduction in marginal tax rates. The relative participation increase of 19.5 percent (9 percentage points) and the relative hours increase of 34.5 percent (206 hours per year) are contaminated by several factors, including a trend component and other contemporaneous demand shocks. Using different control groups reduces these estimates dramatically. Controlling for observable characteristics reduces the estimated participation response further to 8.4 percent using the first control group and 10.9 percent using the second control group. The corresponding response in total labor supply is in the range of 16.9 to 18.4 percent. These estimates are purged of the trend component and any other factors that are common for women whose husbands have less income but not of factors that differ between higher and lower income women, such as changes in the returns to education.

Because women in the 99th percentile of the income distribution are more educated on average than other women, part of their response may be due to higher gross wages rather than to lower taxes. Allowing different responses by more educated women reduces by one half the labor supply effect for the 75th percentile group: all of this effect is operating through the participation decision. There is no analogous effect for the 90th percentile group; this result is not surprising since the difference in average education levels between this control group and the treatment group is only half a year.

The estimates in Eissa (1995a) suggest a total labor supply elasticity between 0.6 and 1 (including both participation and hours of work). Approximately half this response is due to participation. Although the total elasticity estimate is not very different from previous estimates in the literature, its composition is different. Mroz (1987) and Triest (1990) found that hours of work for working women are not affected by the after-tax wage and suggest that the participation decision is responsive to the wage.

In a similar analysis of the ERTA, Eissa (1995b) found a similar overall elasticity but that most of the response to tax reductions results from additional participation. Several differences between the ERTA and TRA can help explain these findings, but the basic explanation is that the 1981 "experiment" is not as clean as the 1986 one. Changes in the income distribution and growth in wage inequality were particularly dramatic in the early 1980s. Moreover, the marginal tax reductions were much larger in 1986 than in 1981. The different results point out a potential problem with the "difference-in-difference" approach, which is that it estimates only the net effect of the policy. I return to this issue in Section 5.

3.2.2 Female Heads of Households Eissa and Liebman (1995) focused on the effects of the TRA and EITC on single women with children. Female heads of households are an important group because they are the largest group of taxpayers eligible for the EITC, making up approximately 48 percent of the EITC-eligible population (Eissa and Liebman, 1993). They identified the impact of the EITC by comparing the change in labor supplied by women with children to the change in labor supplied by women with no children.

Table 3 presents the estimated labor supply response of female heads of households. Eissa and Liebman (1995) found that after the TRA, the labor force participation of single women with children increased by 1.9 to 2.8 percentage points relative to single women without children (from a base of 73.0 percent). They argue that this 2.6 to 3.8 percent increase in participation can be thought of as a response to a $1,100 increase in after-tax income.

Three pieces of evidence suggest that the estimated effect was due to the EITC and not to other parts of the TRA or other government policies. First, in the period that they studied, the amount of EITC a taxpayer received depended only on having a child, and they found that the increase in participation is mostly a response to the return to the first child in the tax unit. The effect of the EITC falls from 3.8 to 3.3 percent once they allow a different response for families with at least two children. Second, the timing of the post-1987 participation increase is consistent with the result being due to the increase in the EITC. Most EITC

TABLE 3
Effects of EITC and TRA of 1986 on Female Heads of Households

Control group	Raw data (%)	Demographic controls (%)	Unemployment rate, AFDC, and state dummy variables added (%)	Second child dummy variable added (%)
Participation response	3.3	2.6	3.8	3.0
Total labor supply	2.1	—	3.0	—

Data are March Current Population Survey 1985–1987 and 1989–1991; see Eissa and Liebman (1995) for details.

recipients would have first become aware of the increase around April of 1988 when they received their 1987 tax refund. If it takes some time to adjust to new incentives, only a limited response should occur in 1988, with a full response in 1989. Eissa and Liebman (1995) found that by 1988, single women with children had increased their relative labor supply by only 1.1 percent, but that in 1989 and 1990, the impact reached 4 percent. Third, Eissa and Liebman (1995) found that the EITC had its largest effect among people most likely to be eligible for the credit. The predicted participation response was approximately 13 percent for women with less than 12 years of schooling and only 0.4 percent for women with more than 12 years of schooling.

Eissa and Liebman (1995) also found no evidence that the EITC expansion had any effect on the hours of work of single women with children who were already in the labor force; the estimates for the total-hours response are similar to the participation responses (Table 3).

3.3 Taxable Income

Other than Bosworth and Burtless (1992), no studies have directly analyzed the male labor supply response to the tax reforms. In this section, I review the evidence on the taxable income response and argue that the large observed responses beg for a direct examination of the male labor supply over the 1980s.

In a series of papers, Lindsey (1987, 1988) examined the income response to the ERTA. He used tax return data from 1979 and the NBER TAXSIM model to impute an income distribution for 1982–1984, and compared that with the actual income distributions for those years. Comparison of two income distributions showed that high-income taxpayers had substantially more income after 1981 in the actual than in the predicted income distribution, whereas low-income taxpayers had less income.

Imputed marginal tax rates showed that the change in the income distribution was consistent with the incentives of the ERTA. Only high-income taxpayers saw a reduction in their marginal rates after the ERTA. Inflation and expansions in the social security payroll offset most of the marginal rate reductions for middle- and low-income individuals. Using elasticities from the literature, Lindsey calculated that at least 40 percent of the response was from increased hours of work, which he estimates at 2.5 percent between 1981 and 1985. The rest is change in the form of compensation (more money wages and fewer untaxed fringe benefits).

Using panel tax return data, Navratil (1994) estimated a taxable response that is substantial but considerably smaller than Lindsey's. He also found that wage income is an important component of that response and concludes that "wage and salary growth may be more the result of supply-side factors than is generally suspected."[12]

Tax return panel data were also used by Feldstein (1995) and Auten and Carroll (1995) to study the taxable income response to the TRA. Feldstein grouped taxpayers by their 1985 marginal tax rate and compared their reported taxable income in 1985 with that in 1988. He estimated a substantial increase in taxable income for upper income taxpayers. Auten and Carroll extended the Feldstein study to account for nontax changes in the economy using data that had a large sample of high-income returns. In addition their data included the occupation of the taxpayer, which they used to control for changes in returns to education and other labor demand factors. They found that half their taxable income response was due to demand factors but still concluded that behavioral responses to the TRA are substantial.

Although the evidence that taxable income responded quite dramatically to the tax reforms is clear, the components of that response are less clear. If we care about the broader dimensions of labor supply (occupational choice, human capital), then the taxable income response is a better measure than hours worked. However, since taxable income includes AGI (wage and salary income, self-employment income, interest, dividends), deductions, and exemptions, it is critical for tax policy that we understand the components of the taxable income response (see Slemrod, 1995).

The evidence that exists shows that both AGI and deductions explain the increase in taxable income at higher incomes (Auten and Carroll, 1995). In addition, the largest source of increase in personal income for the richest individuals between 1984 and 1990 was wages and salaries (45 percent), followed by S corporation income (16.5 percent) and partnerships (Slemrod, 1995).[13]

The key question here is to what extent can the widening wage distri-

---

[12] The difference between the results of Navratil (1994) and Lindsey (1987, 1988) relates to the data used: repeated cross-sectional versus panel data. There are two components to the argument. First, repeated cross-sectional data require that individuals at successive fractiles of the income distribution are essentially the same in 1979 as they are in later years. However, at least 34 percent, and as much as 77 percent, of 1980 taxpayers are in different *deciles* of the taxable income distribution by 1983. Second, repeated cross-sectional data require that individuals be grouped by a variable other than actual marginal tax rates, thus averaging away much of the variation in tax changes within a group. Use of panel data overcomes these problems. These arguments are also relevant for the research on labor supply.

[13] The TRA reduced the top marginal income tax rate below that of the corporate tax rate and made S corporations, which were subject to the individual income tax, more attractive than C corporations, which are subject to the corporate income tax.

bution be explained by changes in labor supply. Although the results in Eissa (1995a,b) suggest a substantial labor supply response by upper income women, they do not explain the widening income distribution for two reasons. First, even though their labor supply response was substantial, there are too few high-income women. Second, women married to men at the top of the income distribution are only weakly attached to the labor force and earn little income, on average. Mean earnings of married women in the highest decile of the other taxable income distribution were $5,100 in 1985 ($11,638 conditional on working) (Navratil, 1994).

Although a voluminous body of work has found that male hours of work and participation are not responsive to economic variables (see Pencavel, 1986), the significant changes in income after the reforms beg the question of whether labor supply (participation and hours worked) responded to tax reforms. Studying male labor supply is therefore important not only for a further understanding of the source of the income response, but for another reason as well. Labor force participation of prime-age men (between the ages of 16 and 48) has declined from 92.7 percent in 1967–1969 to 86.8 percent in 1985–1987. This declining male participation opens the possibility that their participation decision may have become more sensitive to taxation (Heckman, 1993).

4. NEW EVIDENCE ON BEHAVIORAL RESPONSES TO TAX REFORM

In this section, I present evidence on the male labor supply behavior over the past two decades. The goal of this exercise is to examine whether the evidence is consistent with a labor supply response to the tax reforms. The examination of the male labor supply response to the tax reforms is more complicated than that of the female labor supply response. Unlike married women, whose tax treatment is based on a husband's and other household income, and female heads of households, whose tax treatment is based on the presence of a child, the tax treatment of men cannot be so easily determined. To exploit the difference in tax changes for men at different points along the income distribution, education is used as a measure of permanent income and groups men by the number of years of schooling completed. I define four groups: less than 12, 12, 13–16, and more than 16 years of schooling. With this grouping, we can see whether labor supply patterns differed for groups whose incentives were changed in different ways by the ERTA and the TRA. We should expect an increase in labor supplied by men with more than 16 years of education to both the ERTA and TRA, but an increase in labor supplied by men with less than 12 years of schooling only after the TRA. If both of these groups have similar labor supply patterns over both periods, then what we estimate is not a response to tax reform.

Two troubling aspects of grouping by education should be noted at the outset. First, although clearly positively correlated with wages, these education classes explain at most 9 percent of the individual variation in wages. There remains significant variation in wages within each group.[14] Second, returns to education have changed over the same period, making it difficult to isolate the effect of the tax changes. I next discuss the identification of the tax response with the results.

4.1 Data and Sample

I use microdata from the 1977–1994 March CPS.[15] The CPS is a nationally representative data base of approximately 57,000 households.[16] The March data include retrospective income and labor market activity information, so that the data are actually for 1976–1993.

The sample includes heads of tax-filing units[17] between 24 and 55 years old, not ill or disabled or in school or retired. It also excludes men who report negative earned income (wage and salary, farm, and self-employment income) and who report positive earned income but no hours of work for the year. The sample size for all years is 559,592.

Table 4 presents summary statistics for the sample. It also disaggregates the samples by educational attainment. The average man is white, 37 years old, likely to be married, and has completed 1 year of college education. He earns $26,390 (in 1993 dollars). With 96.7 percent probability, he works at least 1 hour during the year, and he works an average of 2,034 hours, 47 weeks per year. The second to fifth columns in Table 4 separate the sample by years of schooling completed (less than 12, 12, 13–16, and more than 16). Again, the idea of separating men by schooling is to isolate groups that are affected differentially by the tax laws. The average man with less than a high school education completes

[14] An alternative strategy might be to predict wage income for each individual and use the predicted income to group individuals. This strategy is problematic because of the extended time period considered and the top coding of income in the CPS.

[15] Before 1977, the CPS reported weeks worked in brackets and provided hours per week only for the reference period (rather than for the previous year). To avoid imputing the variables of interest, I exclude those years.

[16] This number varies over time.

[17] Members of related and unrelated subfamilies residing with the primary family are assumed to file their own tax returns and are allocated to separate filing units.

TABLE 4
Summary Statistics[a]

Variable	All men[b]	Years of schooling completed			
		>12	12	13–16	>16
Age (years)	37.40 (8.91)	39.54 (9.52)	36.92 (8.98)	36.39 (8.52)	38.88 (8.10)
Education (years)[c]	12.94 (3.06)	8.39 (2.47)	12.00 (0)	17.51 (8.46)	17.78 (0.44)
Nonwhite	0.11 (0.32)	0.16 (0.36)	0.11 (0.32)	0.10 (0.30)	0.08 (.28)
Filing unit size	2.84 (1.53)	3.01 (1.71)	2.86 (1.50)	2.74 (1.48)	2.88 (1.49)
Married	0.73 (0.44)	0.75 (0.43)	0.74 (0.44)	0.71 (0.45)	0.76 (0.42)
Personal earned income[d]	$26,390 ($18,366)	$17,360 ($12,638)	$23,382 ($14,305)	$29,313 ($18,708)	$40,899 ($24,529)
Total family income[d]	$35,054 ($23,776)	$22,866 ($15,822)	$30,958 ($18,328)	$39,131 ($24,274)	$54,047 ($31,896)
Annual participation	0.967 (0.178)	0.954 (0.209)	0.964 (0.186)	0.973 (0.161)	0.978 (0.146)
Weekly participation	0.891 (0.247)	0.831 (0.292)	0.887 (0.251)	0.912 (0.226)	0.931 (0.203)
Hours of work	2,034 (731)	1,838 (779)	2,013 (722)	2,094 (697)	2,213 (712)
Observations	559,592	95,528	204,359	196,526	63,179

Source: Data are from the March Current Population Survey (CPS) for years 1977–1994.

[a] Unweighted mean values and standard deviations (in parentheses).

[b] Includes men between the ages of 24 and 55; excludes men who are ill, disabled, in school, or retired and those with negative or positive earned income and zero hours of work.

[c] Calculated using the CPS data from 1977 to 1991; the distribution is calculated for the entire sample.

[d] In 1993 dollars.

only the eighth grade, is 2 years older than the average man, and is less attached to the labor force. In contrast, the average man who has completed college continues his education for almost 2 years (the CPS top codes education at 18 years, so that many of these men might attain more than 2 years of graduate education) and is slightly more attached to the labor force.

4.2 Basic Regression Results

In this section, I present the basic labor supply regression and results. I use three measures of labor supply. The first measure is *annual participation*, defined by whether the individual worked any hours during the year. The other two measures are intended to better capture attachment to the labor force: *percent of weeks worked*, defined as weeks worked divided by 52 (weekly participation) and *annual hours worked*.

The tax laws define three periods over which one can analyze labor supply behavior: 1976–1981 (before tax reform), 1982–1986 (the ERTA), and 1987–1993 (the TRA of 1986). Recall that the ERTA was phased in between 1981 and 1984, whereas the TRA was phased in between 1986 and 1988. If the labor supply response is sluggish, these differences suggest that we are less likely to observe the full response to the ERTA than to the TRA.

To motivate the form of the regressions estimated, consider the factors that may have affected the male labor supply pattern between 1976 and 1993. First, business cycle effects are quite important during this period, especially in the early 1980s. Second, average levels of school completion increased steadily over this period (Murphy and Welch, 1992). The change in the composition of men in the respective education groups over time might also help explain the observed pattern of labor supply.[18] Finally, important changes in the population structure occurred during this time. The peak of the baby boom generation entered the labor market between 1973 and 1980. Change over time in the skill or tastes of successive cohorts conflates the response to taxes.

To address these concerns, I estimate the following equation:

$$l_{it} = f(\alpha_0 + \alpha_1 Q_{it} + \beta \text{ ERTA}_{it} + \gamma \text{ TRA}_{it}), \quad (3)$$

where ERTA is a dummy variable equal to 1 for tax years between 1982 and 1986; TRA is a dummy variable equal to 1 for tax years after 1986 (the excluded period is pre–tax reform); and f is the normal density function in the analysis of participation. The set of controls includes unearned

---

[18] Appendix Tables 1 and 2 present the average characteristics of the sample, classified by education.

TABLE 5
Coefficients from Labor Supply Regressions: Period Dummy Variables

	ERTA (1982–1986)	TRA (1987–1993)
Panel A: Annual Participation (Probit)		
All men	−0.156 (0.11)	−0.014 (0.02)
Education		
Less than high school	−0.289 (0.24)	−0.205 (0.04)
High school	−0.135 (0.18)	0.019 (0.03)
College	−0.113 (0.20)	0.066 (0.03)
Beyond college	−0.086 (0.37)	0.057 (0.06)
Panel B: Weekly Participation (OLS)		
All men	−0.218 (0.001)	−0.003 (0.002)
Education		
Less than high school	−0.425 (0.003)	−0.015 (0.004)
High school	−0.255 (0.002)	0.000 (0.003)
College	−0.108 (0.002)	0.003 (0.003)
Beyond college	−0.005 (0.003)	0.002 (0.004)
Panel C: Total Hours Worked (OLS)		
All men	−67.66 (3.19)	1.13 (4.81)
Education		
Less than high school	−126.02 (7.91)	−62.06 (12.01)
High school	−74.89 (5.27)	12.42 (7.92)
College	−40.78 (5.38)	19.34 (8.11)
Beyond college	−22.50 (9.16)	24.59 (13.83)

Note: Data are from the March Current Population Survey from 1976 to 1993. Regressions include education and education squared for the sample of all men only; age and age squared, unearned income, family size, a dummy variable for marital status (= 1 if married), a dummy variable for race (= 1 if nonwhite), business cycle controls (contemporaneous and lagged gross domestic product growth rate), and cohort dummy variables. Data are presented as mean value (standard error).

income, age and its square, education and its square, marital status, children, race (= 1 if nonwhite), and current and lagged gross domestic product (GDP) growth rates.[19,20]

Panels A–C of Table 5 present the coefficients from regression equation

---

[19] I define eight dummy cohorts: men born during the periods 1921–1930, 1930–1940, 1940–1945, 1945–1950, 1950–1955, 1955–1960, 1960–1965, 1965–1970. The excluded dummy is 1965–1970.

[20] The regressions do not include the hourly wage for two reasons: it is (1) undefined for nonworkers, and (2) measured with error that is negatively correlated with total hours for workers. Because these are reduced-form regressions and the wage is excluded, no meaningful interpretation is attached to the demographic controls in the regressions.

(3) for the entire sample and for samples separated by educational attainment. Panel A presents probit coefficients, and panels B and C present ordinary least squares (OLS) coefficients. The results show a uniform decline in all labor supply measures during the ERTA period, with the most severe decline for men without a high-school degree. The coefficients for the TRA variable show that labor supply remained at levels below the pre–tax reform period for this group (the excluded years in these regressions are 1976–1981). The TRA coefficients for all other groups show an increase in labor supply relative to the pre–tax reform period. Since the change in labor supply relative to the ERTA period determines the size of the TRA effect, these coefficients need to be transformed.

Table 6 reinterprets the results of Table 5. The first column reports the average labor supply for each group in the excluded period, and the second and third columns present the average change in participation after the ERTA and TRA (relative to the previous period). All three panels show marginal effects. Panel A presents the marginal effects calculated from probits of annual participation, and panels B and C present the coefficients from OLS regressions of weekly participation and total annual hours.

After controlling for individual characteristics and business cycle and cohort effects, the results for all men show a labor supply decline of 1.086 percentage points in annual participation (67.66 total hours) in the ERTA period and a rise of 1.178 percentage points (68.79 total hours) in the TRA period for all men.

Different rows in each panel present estimates from regressions that use different samples. Men with less than 12 years of education show a consistently larger decline in all measures after the ERTA than all other groups. All measures of labor supplied by men with less than 12 years of schooling show a rise after the TRA that is smaller than that decline after ERTA, so that by the late 1980s and early 1990s, labor supplied by less educated men is still lower than it had been in the late 1970s. Slightly surprising in Table 6 are the small absolute changes in labor supplied by men with more than 16 years of schooling. This group, however, had the strongest attachment to the labor force to begin with so that smaller absolute responses may not be so surprising. The percent reduction in annual *non*participation by highly educated men is similar to that of male college and high-school graduates (26 versus 28.7 and 24 percent, respectively).

Once relevant factors are controlled for, average changes in labor supply are only weakly correlated with tax changes. Because this approach averages data over many years, however, year effects may bias the results. Year effects derive from shifts in the aggregate labor supply function and from changes over time in wages. To address this issue and to

TABLE 6
Labor Market Participation of Men: Period Dummy Regression Variables

	Pre–tax reform level (1976–1981)	Average change in labor supply relative to previous period	
		ERTA (1982–1986)	TRA (1987–1993)
Panel A: Annual Participation			
All men	96.7	−1.086	1.178
Education			
Less than high school	97.1	−2.591	0.857
High school	96.3	−0.995	1.128
College	96.9	−0.666	1.032
Beyond college	97.1	−0.420	0.688
Panel B: Weekly Participation			
All men	89.3	−2.037	1.976
Education			
Less than high school	86.0	−4.250	2.740
High school	89.2	−2.545	2.549
College	90.7	−1.083	1.357
Beyond College	92.0	−0.484	0.710
Panel C: Total Hours Worked			
All men	2,042.6	−67.66	68.79
Education			
Less than high school	1,929.7	−126.02	63.96
High school	2,038.0	−74.89	87.30
College	2,079.5	−40.78	60.12
Beyond college	2,168.3	−22.50	47.09

Note: Data are from the March Current Population Survey, 1976–1993; participation figures are based on 100 percentage points.

exploit the timing of the responses, I next examine more carefully the trends in labor supply over time.

4.3 Labor Supply Trends

To separate the effects of the tax reforms from those of differential wage growth and aggregate labor supply trends, assume that growing wage inequalities affect the trend from 1976 to 1993 and that the ERTA and TRA affect the trend at 1982 and 1987, respectively. This approach is similar to that used by Bosworth and Burtless (1992) using aggregate data from 1968 to 1990. They allowed one trend starting in 1982. With 6 years of data after 1987, a separate trend for TRA can be estimated.

The estimated regression takes the following form:

$$l_{it} = f(\alpha_0 + \alpha_1 Q_{it} + \beta \text{ Time}_t + \gamma \text{ Time82}_t + \delta \text{ Time87}_t, \quad (4)$$

where Time is a trend starting in 1976; Time82 is a trend starting in 1982; Time87 is a trend starting in 1987. β reflects the patterns in labor supply due to aggregate trends, such as wage growth; and γ and δ reflect the effects of the tax reforms.

Table 7 presents the results. Again, all panels present marginal effects, and different rows present results for different samples, separated by educational attainment. The estimates for all men show a decline in all three measures of participation starting in 1977 and increases starting in 1982 and 1987. Labor force participation by prime-age men increased by 0.113 percentage points per year after the ERTA and by 0.210 percentage points per year after the TRA. Total hours worked fell at a rate of 13.43 per year starting in 1977 and rose by almost 6 hours per year after the ERTA and by an additional 5.7 hours after the TRA.[21]

The rate of decline throughout the period and the rate of increase after the ERTA are generally largest for less educated groups (second and third columns). Annual participation by men with less than 12 years of schooling fell at a rate of 0.351 percentage points per year starting in 1977 and rose by 0.141 percentage points a year after the ERTA and by 0.260 percentage points after the TRA. Total hours worked increased by 6.35 hours per year after the ERTA and by 15.42 hours per year after the TRA. The increase after the ERTA is difficult to interpret because marginal and average rates generally rose for lower income individuals.

A conservative interpretation of these results is that the ERTA trend partially captures the recovery from the recession of the early 1980s and other factors unaccounted for in the regressions but not the tax changes. Even under that interpretation, the evidence suggests a response to the TRA. The labor supply continues to increase after 1986 and in a pattern that is consistent with the marginal tax changes in the TRA. The largest annual responses are by men with less than 12 and more than 16 years of schooling. Between 1987 and 1990, the annual participation rate of the least educated rose by 1.04 percentage points, and total hours worked

---

[21] The hours-of-work results are most comparable to Bosworth and Burtless (1992). By 1989, men worked a total of 130 hours per year more than in 1981. This estimate translates into a 6.5 percent increase in total hours worked compared with 6 percent in the Bosworth and Burtless analysis.

TABLE 7
Labor Market Participation of Men: Time Trend Regressions

	Annual change in labor supply		
	Time (1976–1981)	Time82 (1982–1986)	Time87 (1987–1993)
Panel A: Annual Participation			
All men	−0.141 (0.00)	0.113 (0.00)	0.210 (0.03)
Education			
Less than high school	−0.351 (0.07)	0.141 (0.11)	0.260 (0.09)
High school	−0.142 (0.04)	0.259 (0.07)	0.125 (0.06)
College	−0.047 (0.04)	0.068 (0.06)	0.252 (0.05)
Beyond college	−0.019 (0.06)	0.013 (0.09)	0.295 (0.08)
Panel B: Weekly Participation			
All men	−0.272 (0.04)	0.269 (0.06)	0.208 (0.05)
Education			
Less than high school	−0.466 (0.10)	0.168 (0.16)	0.546 (0.14)
High school	−0.431 (0.04)	0.535 (0.10)	0.128 (0.86)
College	−0.013 (0.06)	0.090 (0.09)	0.112 (0.07)
Beyond college	0.153 (0.10)	−0.249 (0.15)	0.290 (0.12)
Panel C: Total Hours Worked			
All men	−13.43 (1.11)	15.83 (1.71)	5.71 (1.37)
Education			
Less than high school	−17.41 (2.60)	6.35 (4.24)	15.42 (3.68)
High school	−17.20 (1.84)	22.18 (2.85)	4.13 (2.29)
College	−7.77 (1.90)	14.36 (2.87)	2.15 (2.21)
Beyond college	−3.38 (3.28)	7.26 (5.03)	7.76 (4.02)

Note: Data are from the March Current Population Survey, 1976–1993. Regressions include education and education squared for the sample of all men only; age and age squared, unearned income, family size, a dummy variable for marital status (= 1 if married), a dummy variable for race (= 1 if nonwhite), business cycle controls (contemporaneous and lagged GDP growth rate), and cohort dummy variables. Participation figures are based on 100 percentage points. Data are presented as mean value (standard error).

Time, pre–tax reform; Time82, Economic Recovery Tax Act of 1981; Time87, Tax Reform Act of 1986.

increased by 61.6 hours per year. For the most educated group, annual participation rose by 1.2 percentage points and total hours worked rose by 31 hours per year.

4.4 Alternative Specifications

The previous estimates are preferable to the initial estimates because they use the timing of the tax laws to identify the response. However, they are restrictive in that they impose linear trends. An even more

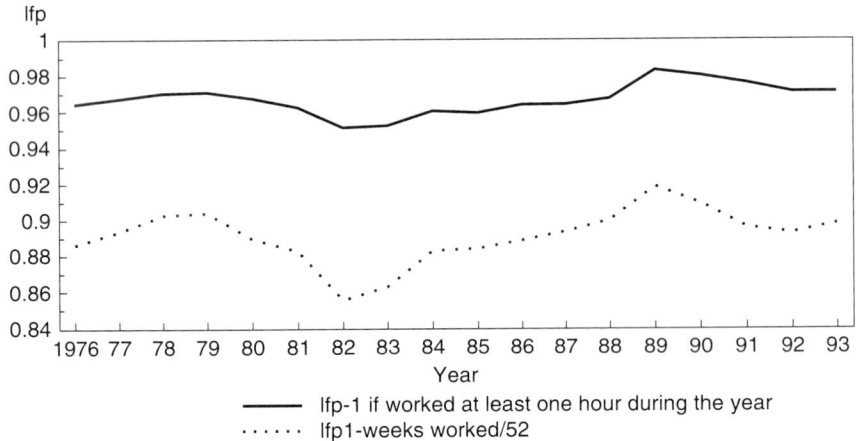

FIGURE 1. *Labor force participation rate, 1976–1993.*

flexible method of analyzing the response is to plot labor supply trends over time. Figure 1 presents the average (annual and weekly) participation rate of men between 1976 and 1993. The two measures have different mean values but show similar patterns. The effect of the recession in the early 1980s is evident from the data; the participation rate falls from 1979 to 1982, after which the recovery starts. Figure 1 suggests that it is difficult to disentangle the effect of the ERTA from the effect of the recession because of the timing of the tax law; however, the effect of the TRA is clearer.

To purge the trend from the effects of changes in observable characteristics and cohort effects, I estimate regressions with 17-year dummy variables and the same observable characteristics included in previous regressions. Separate regressions are estimated for each education group. The marginal effects calculated from the coefficients for the year dummy variables are plotted in Figures 2 and 3. Several observations are clear. First, the significant heterogeneity across groups in the labor supply trend is apparent. The least educated group showed no increase in labor supply after 1987; in fact, the labor supply declined. Predicted labor market participation by men with less than 12 years of education never fully recovered from the recession of the early 1980s. Between 1978 and 1982, the GDP growth rate fell by 7 percentage points, from 4.5 to −2.5. Labor force participation by men with less than 12 years of education fell by more than 4 percentage points.

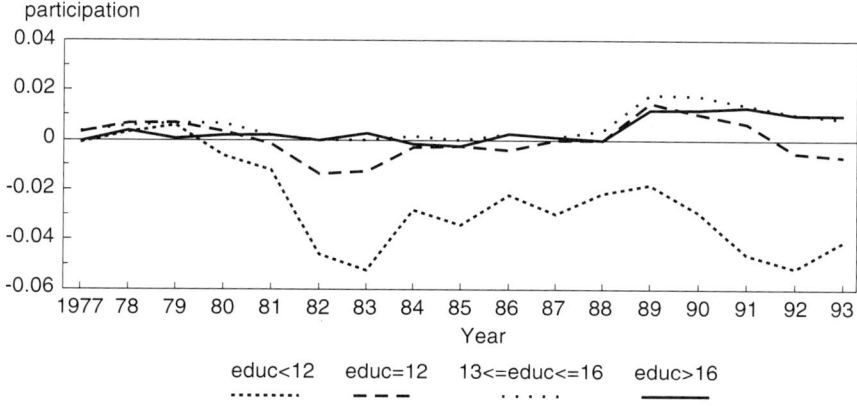

FIGURE 2. *Marginal effects: probability of participation, 1977–1993.*

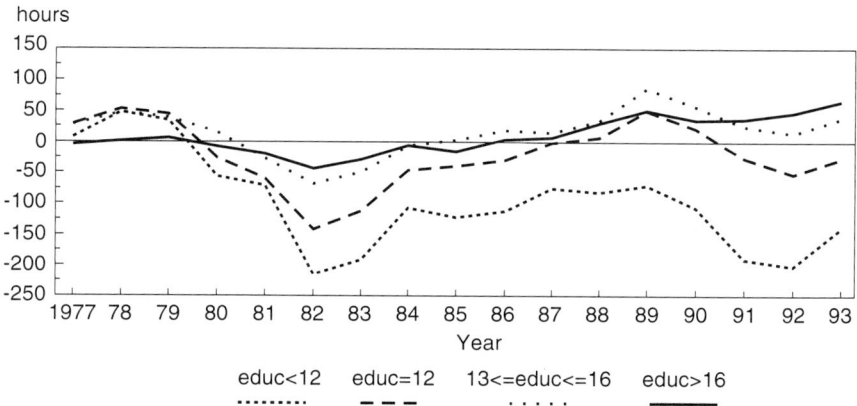

FIGURE 3. *Coefficients of year dummy variables: annual hours, 1977–1993.*

The participation rate of men with more than 12 years of education shows some responsiveness to the TRA: it jumps between 1 and 2 percentage points in 1987. Although we observe similar jumps in participation rates by men with 12 years of schooling, their participation immediately declines starting in 1988. No such jumps in hours worked are observed for the most educated men, which is the only group that does not show any decline in total hours worked after 1989 (Figure 3). Overall, Figures 1–3 suggest that evidence of a male labor supply response to the tax reforms is quite weak.

5. DISCUSSION AND CONCLUSION

The tax reforms of the 1980s provided economists with a remarkable opportunity to evaluate individual behavioral responses to tax reforms. This paper has reviewed the evidence from the literature and presented new evidence on individual behavioral responses to tax reforms.

It is useful to conclude by considering what we have *not* learned from the evidence summarized and presented in this paper. Studies that directly analyzed the labor supply present evidence that the female labor supply is responsive to taxes. The question that arises is, What parameters do these studies estimate?[22] The "difference-in-difference" approach estimates the net response to the tax reforms, which amounts to the uncompensated response. Generally, then, we have not learned from this evidence the preference parameters needed to evaluate tax reforms. There are exceptions, however. The results in Eissa (1995a) may be interpreted as compensated labor supply elasticities, since the TRA had a small income effect. Still, none of the work has isolated the income elasticity of hours worked or participation.[23] Separating the income and substitution effects requires more structural modeling of labor supply behavior and stronger assumptions about functional form (see Blundell, Duncan, and Meghir, 1995).[24]

---

[22] In principle, the change in labor supply after the tax reforms includes intertemporal substitution and income and substitution effects. Individuals may intertemporally substitute labor supply if they foresee the tax change, or if they believe it to be temporary. Both the ERTA and TRA were phased in over time, and so we should expect that some intertemporal substitution in labor supply occurred. However, several reasons suggest that the intertemporal substitution effects will be small. Using data on hours worked, empirical labor supply research shows little intertemporal substitution (see Heckman, 1993). Also, Hausman and Poterba (1987) argue that the after-tax rate of return is not substantially affected for many households. In a life-cycle model of labor supply, both the path of after-tax wages and after-tax returns matter for labor supply decisions. A stronger reason to suspect that we estimate a long-run response is that the studies cover periods that completely bracket the tax changes.

[23] The income effect is necessary for applied welfare analysis if taxpayers are making a discrete choice, such as whether or not to participate in the labor force (Small and Rosen, 1981).

[24] Blundell, Duncan, and Meghir (1995) estimate a structural model of labor supply that identifies the income and substitution effects from the tax reforms that took place in England over the 1980s. The reforms raised and lowered rates during the 1980s. Blundell, Duncan, and Meghir use these changes, along with the change in returns to education that varied by cohorts, to identify the income and wage effects of the tax reform. Applying their

There is an important trade-off here. Although structural models of labor supply yield preference parameters that can be used for welfare analysis of tax reform, they have been widely criticized for the restrictive assumptions imposed (MaCurdy, Green, and Paarsch, 1990) and for their sensitivity to the preference and model specifications used (Heckman, 1982; Triest, 1990). By focusing on affected groups and using arguably more exogenous variation in marginal rates, the natural experiment approach minimizes the potential for functional form assumptions to bias the results.[25] Difference-in-difference approaches rely on more transparent assumptions to identify the tax effect. The advantage of that strategy is that the direction and size of any biases become transparent. The disadvantage is that it generally does not yield the preference parameters.

Building on the evidence that shows an increase in taxable income by higher income individuals after the tax reforms, the current paper also analyzed whether those responses were due to an increase in male labor market participation. Although high-income married women have been shown to be quite sensitive to the changes in marginal rates, their increased labor supply does not explain the large increase in income observed in tax return data. Women married to high-income men do not earn enough to explain the surge in income.

Microdata from 1976 to 1993 show only weak evidence of a small increased male labor supply response after the TRA of 1986. For men with 16 years of schooling, the trend regressions show an increase in total hours of work of about 50 hours per year, or 2 percent. This response is much smaller than what the studies on the income response suggest (Feenberg and Poterba, 1993; Auten and Carroll, 1995; Feldstein, 1995; Slemrod, 1995) and suggest that the income response observed in the tax return data is due more to factors other than labor market participation, such as shifting of income and compensation decisions. Finally, one cannot conclude from this evidence that the labor supply of men more broadly defined to include work effort, occupational choice, and human capital accumulation, showed little response to the tax reforms.

---

approach to the United States would be very involved because the U.S. tax code is far more complicated than the British tax code.

[25] For example, one does not need to use after-tax wages in the regression, which are measured with error in survey data (Mroz, 1987); neither does one need to impute wages for individuals out of the labor force.

APPENDIX TABLE 1
Summary Statistics for All Men[a]

Variable	1976–1993	Pre–tax reform	ERTA	TRA
Age (years)	37.40 (8.91)	37.35 (9.25)	37.08 (8.88)	37.67 (8.62)
Education (years)	12.94 (3.06)	12.71 (3.16)	13.04 (3.01)	NA
Less than high school (%)	17.1	21.0	16.5	14.1
High school (%)	36.5	36.4	37.4	36.0
Beyond high school (%)	35.1	42.5	46.0	50.0
Nonwhite	0.11 (0.32)	0.10 (0.30)	0.11 (0.31)	0.12 (0.33)
Filing unit size	2.84 (1.53)	3.04 (1.59)	2.81 (1.51)	2.69 (1.48)
Married	0.73 (0.44)	0.780 (0.414)	0.730 (0.444)	0.697 (0.460)
Observations	559,592	183,561	155,928	220,103

Source: Data are from the March Current Population Survey (CPS) from survey years 1977–1994 and are presented as mean value (standard deviation); data collected for the year prior to survey year.

[a] Includes men between ages 24 and 55 and excludes men who were ill, disabled, in school, or retired and those with negative or positive earned income and zero hours of work.

NA, not available; CPS changed education codes in 1991.

APPENDIX TABLE 2
Summary Statistics for All Men by Education[a]

Variable	1976–1993	Pre–tax reform	ERTA	TRA
Less than high school				
Age (years)	39.54 (9.52)	41.69 (9.47)	39.29 (9.59)	38.30 (9.36)
Education (years)	8.39 (2.47)	8.34 (2.43)	8.45 (2.45)	NA
Nonwhite (%)	0.16 (0.36)			
Filing unit size (no.)	3.01 (1.71)	3.24 (1.78)	2.96 (1.66)	2.77 (1.61)
Married (no.)	0.75 (0.43)	0.803 (0.398)	0.746 (0.435)	0.683 (0.465)
Observations (no.)	95,528	38,779	25,793	30,956
Beyond college				
Age (years)	38.88 (8.10)	37.5 (8.24)	38.7 (7.99)	40.2 (7.85)
Education (years)	17.78 (0.44)	17.7 (0.451)	17.7 (0.438)	NA
Nonwhite (%)	0.08 (.28)			
Filing unit size (no.)	2.89 (1.49)	2.99 (1.54)	2.85 (1.47)	2.82 (1.46)
Married (no.)	0.76 (0.42)	0.777 (0.417)	0.756 (0.429)	0.760 (0.427)
Observations (no.)	63,179	20,421	18,678	24,080

Source: Data are from the March Current Population Survey (CPS) from survey years 1977–1994 and are presented as mean value (standard deviation).

[a] Includes men between ages 24 and 55 and excludes men who were ill, disabled, in school, or retired and those with negative or positive earned income or zero hours of work.

NA, not available; CPS changed education codes in 1991.

REFERENCES

Auten, Gerald, and Robert Carroll (1995). "Taxpayer Behavior and the 1986 Tax Reform Act." Treasury Department, Office of Tax Analysis. Mimeograph.

Blundell, Richard, Alan Duncan, and Costas Meghir (1995). "Estimating Labor Supply Responses Using Tax Reforms." The Institute for Fiscal Studies. Mimeograph.

Bosworth, Barry, and Gary Burtless (1992). "Effects of Tax Reform on Labor Supply, Investment, and Saving." *Journal of Economic Perspectives* 6(no. 1):3–26.

Deloitte and Touche (1993). "Shifting the Burden; The 1993 Tax Changes." Deloitte, Touche, Tohmatsu: International.

Eissa, Nada (1995a). "Taxation and Labor Supply of Married Women: The Tax Reform Act of 1986 as a Natural Experiment." NBER Working Paper no. 5023.

———. (1995b). "Labor Supply Response to the Economic Recovery Tax Act of 1981." Paper presented at NBER Conference on Tax Policy Analysis, Islamoradaadora, FL, January.

———, and Jeffrey B. Liebman (1995). "Labor Supply Response to the Earned Income Tax Credit." NBER Working Paper no. 5158. Forthcoming in *Quarterly Journal of Economics*.

Feenberg, Daniel, and James Poterba (1993). "Income Inequality and the Incomes of Very High Income Taxpayers." In *Tax Policy and the Economy*, vol. 7, pp. 145–177, James Poterba (ed.). Cambridge, MA: MIT Press.

Feldstein, Martin (1995). "The Effect of Marginal Tax Rates on Taxable Income: A Panel Study of the 1986 Tax Reform Act." *Journal of Political Economy.* Vol. 103, no. 3, pp. 551–572.

———, and Andrew Samwick (1992). "Social Security Rules and Marginal Tax Rates." *National Tax Journal* 45 (no. 1):1–22.

Hausman, Jerry (1981). "Labor Supply." In *How Taxes Affect Economic Behavior,* Henry Aaron and Joseph Pechman (eds.). Washington, DC: The Brookings Institution.

———. (1985). "Taxes and Labor Supply." In *Handbook of Public Economics,* Vol. I, Alan Auerbach and Martin Feldstein (eds.). Amsterdam: Elsevier.

———, and James Poterba (1987). "Household Behavior and the Tax Reform Act of 1986." *Journal of Economic Perspectives* 1(no. 1):101–120.

Heckman, James. (1993). "What Has Been Learned About Labor Supply in the Past Twenty Years?" *American Economic Review* 83(no. 2):116–121.

———, and Mark Killingsworth. "Female Labor Supply." In *Handbook of Labor Economics.* Vol. I. Orley Ashenfelter and Richard Layard (eds.). Amsterdam: Elsevier.

Juhn, Chin-hui (1992). "Decline of Male Labor Market Participation: The Role of Declining Market Opportunities." *Quarterly Journal of Economics* Vol. 107, no. 1, pp. 79–121.

Katz, Lawrence, and Kevin Murphy (1992). "Changes in Relative Wages, 1963–1987: Supply and Demand Factors." *Quarterly Journal of Economics* 107(no. 1):35–78.

Lindsey, Lawrence. (1987). "Individual Taxpayer Response to Tax Cuts, 1982–1984: With Implications for the Revenue Maximizing Tax Rate." *Journal of Public Economics* 33:173–206.

———. (1988). "Did ERTA Raise the Share of Taxes Paid by Upper-Income Taxpayers? Will TRA86 Be a Repeat?" In *Tax Policy and the Economy,* Vol. 2, Lawrence Summer (ed.). Cambridge: MIT Press, 131–160.

MaCurdy, Thomas, David Green, and Harry Paarsch (1990). "Assessing Empirical Approaches for Analyzing Taxes and Labor Supply." *The Journal of Human Resources* 25(no. 3):415–490.

Mroz, Thomas (1987). "Sensitivity of an Empirical Model of Married Women's Hours of Work to Economic and Statistical Assumptions." *Econometrica* 55(no. 4):765–799.

Murphy, Kevin, and Finis Welch (1992). "The Structure of Wages." *Quarterly Journal of Economics* 107(no. 1):285–326.

Navratil, John (1994). "Evidence of Individual Taxpayer Behavior from Panel Tax Return Data." Harvard University. Mimeograph.

Pechman, Joseph (1987). *Federal Tax Policy.* Washington, DC: The Brookings Institution.

Pencavel, John (1986). "Labor Supply of Men: A Survey." In *Handbook of Labor Economics,* Vol. I, Orley Ashenfelter and Richard Layard (eds.). Amsterdam: Elsevier.

Slemrod, Joel (1995). "High-Income Families and the Tax Changes of the 1980's: The Anatomy of Behavioral Response." NBER Working Paper no. 5218.

Small, Kenneth, and Harvey Rosen (1981). "Applied Welfare Analysis With Discrete Choice Models." *Econometrica,* Vol. 49, no. 1, pp. 105–130.

Triest, Ronald (1990). "The Effect of Income Taxation on Labor Supply in the United States." *The Journal of Human Resources* 25(no. 3):491–516.
———. 1992. "The Effect of Income Taxation on Labor Supply When Deductions Are Endogenous." *The Review of Economics and Statistics* 25(no. 3):91–99.